THE
BIBLE BRIEF:

A Compact Summary Of The 66 Books That Changed The World – A Bible Study & Reference Guidebook

By

James Paris

Published By

Deanburn Publications

Table of Contents

Contents

Acts: 101

Romans: 104

1 Corinthians: 106

2 Corinthians: 108

Galatians: 110

Ephesians: 113

Philippians: 115

Colossians: 116

1 Thessalonians: 118

2 Thessalonians: 120

1 Timothy: 122

2 Timothy: 124

Titus: 126

Philemon: 128

Hebrews: 130

James: 132

1 Peter: 134

2 Peter: 136

1 John: 138

2 John: 140

3 John: 141

Jude: 143

Revelation: 144

Permissions/Copyright

Scripture taken from the NEW AMERICAN STANDARD BIBLE ®,

Copyright © 1960,1962,1963,1968, 1971,1973,1975,1977,1995 by The Lockman Foundation.

Used by permission

Copyright 2012, James Paris

All rights reserved. Copyright protected. Duplicating, reprinting or distributing this material for commercial purposes without the express written consent of the author is prohibited.

While reasonable attempts have been made to assure the accuracy of the information contained within this publication, the author does not assume any responsibility for errors, omissions or contrary interpretation of this information, and any damages incurred by that.

The author does not assume any responsibility or liability whatsoever, for what you choose to do with this information.

www.deanburnpublications.com

Introduction:

The Bible In Brief; is a summary of all the 66 books that make up the Bible as we know it today. Written as an aid to Bible study, or a handy 'bite sized' reference book; this Bible guidebook gives an overall view, listing the main points of the individual books involved.

Through all these 66 books, and the lives and trials of the characters within, I believe our Creator has one main thing to say – he loves us with a love that is beyond our comprehension to fully appreciate. The Bible is God's plan for our redemption and a history of his dealings with us – "warts & all." This is no 'sugar coated' work of some religious idealist; but rather is an account from many different individuals such as Kings, Prophets, Shepherds, Farmers etc; that records all the bad and ugly side of human nature; and yet still declares Gods love for us through the sacrifice of His Son Jesus Christ.

That said, there is a huge amount of information contained within the pages of the Bible; too much to be absorbed at one sitting so to speak. It is for this reason that 'The Bible Brief' was written; to enable an overview of the individual books so that when time or circumstances permit you can go to the Bible itself and read the story in full – which I would recommend whole-heartedly!

The Bible Brief includes facts such as the time of writing and the author of the book, along with main characters involved, and some memorable scriptures are covered; along with a short summary of the book itself, and some 'Notes & Quotes' that may express my own views or input.

Perhaps most importantly the 'Messianic Link' section covers some of the messianic scriptures that unite all the 66 books. These are the scriptures that refer either directly or indirectly to the coming Messiah; recording everything from the prophesied virgin birth to the resurrection and the second coming of Christ in power.

1. WHEN: The date of the book was written or the time period covered.
2. WHO: The author or presumed author of the book.
3. PEOPLE & PLACES: The 'main players' & places involved or referred to.
4. SOUND-BITES: Memorable quotes, sayings or verses from the book.
5. THE MESSIANIC LINK: The coming Messiah is mentioned throughout - and ties together - the 66 books. These are just some of the scriptures that allude to or name the Messiah directly.
6. THE BOOK: An outline of the book or letter.
7. NOTES & QUOTES: General thoughts & comments on the preceding book.

The Bible is indeed a book worth knowing, let The Bible Brief introduce it (and commend it) to you.

OLD TESTAMENT
(Covenant)

INTRO:

The 'Old Testament' or 'Covenant,' actually refers to the covenant that God had with the Jews. This was a covenant or pact that they had with God based on their ability to appease Him with blood sacrifice; religious and legal observance. Covering the first 39 books of the Bible, it lays the foundation and prepares the way for the New Covenant to come.

Genesis:

WHEN:

Written at the time of Moses around 1445-1406B.C.

WHO:

Generally attributed to Moses, but with events recorded much further back in time.

PEOPLE & PLACES:

Adam & Eve; Cain & Abel; Methuselah; Enoch; Abraham; Isaac; Jacob (Israel); Ishmael; Rachael; Esau; Joseph; Pharaoh.
The Garden of Eden; Babel; Egypt; Sodom & Gomorrah; Salem; Canaan

SOUND-BITES:

Then God said, "Let there be light"; and there was light.(Gen 1:3)

Then the Lord God formed man of dust from the ground, and breathed into his nostrils the breath of life; and man became a living being. (Gen 2:7)

"No longer shall your name be called Abram,
But your name shall be Abraham;
For I have made you the father of a multitude of nations. (Gen 15:5)

But his wife, from behind him, looked back, and she became a pillar of salt. (Gen 19:26)
As for you, you meant evil against me, but God meant it for good in order to bring about this present result, to preserve many people alive. (Gen 50:20)

THE MESSIANIC LINK:
Messiah would be born of the seed of a woman (Gen 3:15)
Descendant of Abraham, Isaac & Jacob. (Gen 12:3, 17:19, 28:14).
He would come from the royal line of Judah (Gen 49:10, John 1:49)
Isaac represented him in Genesis 22
He was typified in Joseph in Genesis 37

THE BOOK:
The story of Genesis is one of the creation of the universe and all living things; to the subsequent rebellion and fall of man and the redemption offered by God through the coming messiah.

Sin enters through the eating of the fruit of the 'tree of the knowledge of good and evil' in the garden – something which had been expressly forbidden by God, and through it the expulsion from the garden of Eden and the first murder by Adam's son Cain off his brother Abel.

Mankind is condemned thereafter to struggle with sin and death, whilst awaiting the promised redemption in the form of a Messianic Saviour (Gen 3:15).

The whole Earth is flooded to destroy all but Noah and his family in chapter 7, and the Tower of Babel is built – and the people scattered - in chapter 11.

Throughout the book of Genesis we see the birth and growth of the human race, from the early days of Adam & Eve to the later chapters where we see the entrance of the Patriarchs Abraham, Isaac and Jacob – later Called Israel; and the entry into exile in Egypt.

NOTES & QUOTES:

Genesis is the first of the five books of the Pentateuch, each being mainly attributed to Moses.

There are many people today who would seek to place the book of Genesis firmly in the field of mythology; this would be a great mistake. This book offers Christians (and the rest of the world) an explanation for the mess that we now all in; in a word SIN. To treat the book of Genesis as anything other than the divinely inspired Word of God is to fall into error. Remove Genesis and you remove the concept of sin, and there-fore the need of a saviour.

It is natural for Satan to try this line of attack, for the best way to collapse a building is to erode away the foundation.

Genesis is the foundation of the Bible, to remove it is to collapse the building.

This is a strong book, easily able to defend itself – even against the pseudo-science of evolution; now itself on the back-foot with the revelations of genetic science and the move towards 'creationism'.

******

Exodus:

WHEN:
Around The time of Moses 1445-1406 B.C.

WHO:
Attributed to Moses c.f. Exodus Ch.17:14 or Ch.34:27

PEOPLE & PLACES:
Moses; Aaron; Jethro; Pharaoh
Egypt; Midian; Canaan; Mount Sinai

SOUND-BITES:

Now a new king arose over Egypt, who did not know Joseph.(Ex 1:8)

But he said, "Who made you a prince or a judge over us? Are you intending to kill me as you killed the Egyptian?" (Ex.2:14)

But Moses said before the Lord, "Behold, I am unskilled in speech; how then will Pharaoh listen to me?" (Ex 6:30)

"You shall have no other gods before Me." (Ex 20:3)

But He said, "You cannot see My face, for no man can see Me and live!" (Ex 33:20)

THE MESSIANIC LINK:
The Messiah is typified in the life of Moses.
The Passover Lamb of Exodus 12
The Manna from heaven in Ch.16
The rock that was struck at Horeb in Ch.17

THE BOOK:
The main story in the book of Exodus is of course the departure of the Israelites from slavery in Egypt and the subsequent 40 years in the desert wilderness of the Sinai. After being led there to avoid famine in Joseph's time, they had become slaves after Joseph dies, and a new Pharaoh who did not know Joseph takes command. (Ch.1:8)
The feast of the Passover is inaugurated during this time as God spares the Israelite children from the angel of death that destroys the first-born of the Egyptians.
The episode of the burning bush (Ch.3:1-6), the partings of the Red sea, and the destruction of the Egyptian army; as well as the pillar of smoke by day and fire by night to lead the people, are notable events.
Here also we see the beginning of the priesthood, and the building and setting up of the Tabernacle. The Ten Commandments are set up (Ch. 20) and the worship of the golden calf brings down the wrath of God in chapter 32. Chapter 35 sees the setting up of the Sabbath day as a day of rest.

In chapter 40 we see the Tabernacle erected and the Glory of The Lord filling the temple.

NOTES & QUOTES:

The book of Exodus, apart from being an historical record of how God rescued his people from the Egyptians; is a record of Redemption and Deliverance. As such it is symbolical of the way in which The Lord has delivered us from the bondage of sin, and freed us through the sacrificial offering of The Lord Jesus at Calvary.

******

<u>Leviticus:</u>

WHEN:

Time is set by Leviticus 1:1 which states that God spoke to Moses. This places the writing between 1445 – 1406 B.C.

WHO:

It is made clear from the beginning, and from more than 50 other places throughout, that Moses wrote the book.

PEOPLE & PLACES:

Moses; Aaron; Nadab; Abihu

SOUND-BITES:

Thus Aaron and his sons did all the things which the Lord had commanded through Moses. (Ch.8:36)

"For the life of the flesh is in the blood,…" (Ch.17:11)

Do not turn to idols or make for yourselves molten gods; I am the Lord your God. (Ch.19:4)

I will also walk among you and be your God, and you shall be My people. (Ch.26:12)

THE MESSIANIC LINK:

Messiah is typified in the sacrifices & Offerings
He is the High priest.
The scapegoat of Ch.16; who takes away the sins of the people.

THE BOOK:

The book of Leviticus (meaning, relating to the Levites) is written to instruct the people on Holiness, and just what it takes to be considered acceptable in the eyes of God.
A book on instruction regarding sacrifice and bodily cleanliness, peace offerings, grain offerings, guilt offerings and many more are all covered in this book.
Punishments to suit the individual crimes are all set out, including the punishment for immoral relationships (Ch.18) Idolatry (Ch.19) and Human sacrifice.

NOTES & QUOTES:

This book along with Deuteronomy is perhaps the most unread book in the whole Bible! Being as it is, full of rules and regulations that seem alien to modern day Christians; and in many ways this is indeed so. However it nevertheless plays an important role in the understanding of the need for a Messiah or saviour, as it points out just how impossible it is to be acceptable to God without the intervention of our own High Priest – Jesus.

******

Numbers:

WHEN:
The time of Moses 1445-1406 B.C.

WHO:
Moses

PEOPLE & PLACES:
Moses; Aaron; Joshua; Eleazar; Balaam; Joshua; Miriam; Caleb; Korah
Sinai; Canaan; Kadesh; Moab; Meribah; Jordan

SOUND-BITES:
Just as the Lord had commanded Moses. So he numbered them in the wilderness of Sinai. (Ch.1:19)

The Lord bless you, and keep you;
The Lord make His face shine on you, And be gracious to you;
The Lord lift up His countenance on you,
And give you peace.' (Ch.6:24-26)

Now the man Moses was very humble, more than any man who was on the face of the earth. (Ch.12:3)

"…and be sure your sin will find you out." (Ch32:23)

THE MESSIANIC LINK:
He is the pillar of Cloud and Fire. (Ch.14:14)
The Star that comes forth from Jacob. (Ch.24:17)

He is typified in the story of the bronze serpent. (Ch.21:8-9)

The Water that springs from the Rock. (Ch.20)

THE BOOK:

This book gets its name from the fact that it begins and ends with a census of the people, when the Israelite population is 'numbered' and their military strength assessed.

By the time of the second census 38 years had passed by, and all of the people that had originally left Egypt were no more – with the exception of Joshua and Caleb.

This book is concerned particularly with the grumbling nature of the Israelites; even the manna from heaven that The Lord provided, did not satisfy them!

When they refused to enter the land of the Canaanites out of fear of the natives, thereby disobeying God despite the urgings of Joshua and Caleb; The Lord condemned them to walk the desert until they had all perished. Only Joshua and Caleb out of the entire host would enter the 'promised land.'

Rebellion against God and Moses by the people, led to them being chastised with Fiery Serpents (Ch.21:5-6). Moses himself finally fell afoul of the Wrath of God by striking the Rock twice at the wilderness of Zin; when he was told just to speak to it. In this act, he did not give The Lord the respect that he was due (Ch.20:12). As promised, he never set foot in the 'promised land' though God did allow him to see it before he died. (Deut 34:1-7)

NOTES & QUOTES:

If anything, this book tells us that The Lord is Holy, and that he is to be taken at his word; no matter how insurmountable the barriers may seem or how strong the opposition may be. When God opens the door, then no man can close it.

Another lesson is perhaps even harder to put into practice – beware of grumbling! The rebellion of Korah (Ch.16:2-3), or Aaron and Miriam (Ch.12:9-10), had drastic consequences for those involved.

******

Deuteronomy:

WHEN:
The time of Moses 1445-1406 B.C. Near the time of his death.

WHO:
Moses. (cf. Ch.1:5; 31:9,22,24)

PEOPLE & PLACES:
Moses; Aaron; Joshua
Jordan; The Red Sea; Moab; Horeb; Canaan; Cities of Refuge

SOUND-BITES:
"These are the words which Moses spoke…" (Ch.1:1)

"Be strong and courageous, do not be afraid or tremble at them, for the Lord your God is the one who goes with you. He will not fail you or forsake you." (Ch.31:6)

But you shall remember the Lord your God, for it is He who is giving you power to make wealth, that He may confirm His covenant which He swore to your fathers, as it is this day. (Ch.8:18)

THE MESSIANIC LINK:
Messiah will be a Prophet like Moses. (Ch18:18)
He is typified in the cities of refuge. (Ch.4:41-43)

THE BOOK:
Deuteronomy is all about repetition and re-enforcement, for indeed the word 'Deuteronomy' can be translated as 'Repetition of the law.'
Moses takes the occasion here, near the end of his life to write down and re-enforce the laws and statutes, lest the people forget what has happened when they disobeyed in the past! Remembering that by this time, almost all of the original exiles had perished, and so memories of the past events were no longer fresh.
The love of God for his people is emphasised, and the Ten Commandments repeated (Ch.5).
Before Moses passes on to 'sleep with his fathers' he assures his people that the love of God and his guidance will continue through Joshua (Ch.31:1-34:12), and the obedience to Gods commandments.

NOTES & QUOTES:

Although many readers will throw up their arms in despair, at the thought of ploughing through Deuteronomy! It is nevertheless an important book, even for New Testament Christians. It is quoted some 80 times through-out the New Testament's 27 books, which alone is cause enough to persevere when reading it. We are now under Grace rather than the Law, thankfully. However by reading this last book of Moses, we may come to a better overall understanding of the events that have shaped where we are today-by God's Grace.

******

<u>Joshua:</u>

WHEN:
Not exactly determined, but before 1000 B.C.

WHO:
According to tradition, Joshua himself is believed to have written the book; possibly with input from Eleazar and Samuel.

PEOPLE & PLACES:
Joshua (Hoshe'a); Caleb; Rahab; Achan
Jordan; Canaan; Jericho; Ai; Lebanon; Gibeon; Mount Gaash

SOUND-BITES:

"Moses My servant is dead; now therefore arise, cross this Jordan, you and all this people, to the land which I am giving to them, to the sons of Israel." (Ch.1:2)

"Remove your sandals from your feet, for the place where you are standing is holy." (Ch.5:15)

..and when the people heard the sound of the trumpet, the people shouted with a great shout and the wall fell down flat. (Ch.6:20)

THE MESSIANIC LINK:
Joshua is a 'type' of Messiah
Jesus is The Christians 'Promised Land'

THE BOOK:
The book of Joshua begins with the death of Moses according to the word of The Lord (Deut 32:52) and continues with the conquest and occupation of the Promised Land of Canaan. Rahab the harlot gains the two Israelite spies access into the city of Jericho, thereby saving herself and her family from destruction when the walls of Jericho miraculously collapse.
Canaan is divided amongst the 12 tribes (Ch.13) and the six cities of refuge built (Ch.20).
Joshua renews the Israelites commitment to The Lord, before he died and was buried at Timnath-serah in Ephraim, after reaching the ripe old age of 110. (Ch.2)

NOTES & QUOTES:
This book is probably best known for the stories of Rahab the harlot, and the miraculous collapsing of the walls of

Jericho. There has been much conjecture and speculation regarding this event. Personally I believe it should be simply seen as a miraculous intervention of God; why should it be treated any different from the hundreds if not thousands of other miracles throughout the Bible?

******

Judges:

WHEN:
Covers time between 1400 – 1050 B.C. Most probably written or compiled around 800B.C.

WHO:
According to tradition Samuel wrote the book of Judges, though scholars generally agree as to input from other sources.

PEOPLE & PLACES:
Joshua; Deborah; Barak; Gideon; Samson; Delilah
Canaan; Judah; Hebron; Gaza; Shechem

SOUND-BITES:
The Lord said, "Judah shall go up; behold, I have given the land into his hand." (Ch.1:2)

He said to Him, "O Lord, how shall I deliver Israel? Behold, my family is the least in Manasseh, and I am the youngest in my father's house." (Ch.6:15)

"With the jawbone of a donkey, Heaps upon heaps,

With the jawbone of a donkey I have killed a thousand men." (Ch.15:16)

In those days there was no king in Israel; every man did what was right in his own eyes. (Ch.17:6)

THE MESSIANIC LINK:
Jesus is typified throughout the book of Judges as he is the true and righteous Judge of all the earth.

THE BOOK:
The book of Judges covers a period when there was no King in Israel (Ch.17:6). Rebellion was commonplace as was murder, rape, and idolatry (Ch.2:12). The people had become backslidden shortly after the death of Joshua, and this led to unrest and disillusionment; which in turn led to the appointing of Judges to guide them through particularly turbulent periods.

Heroes of the book include Gideon (Ch.6:12) whom the Lord raised up to become a mighty commander; and of course Samson (Ch.14) whom the Lord raised to champion them against the Philistines.

The tribe of Benjamin is almost completely destroyed in a civil war (Ch.20), that resulted from the gang-rape and murder of a Levites concubine in Gibeah – a city of the Benjamites.

NOTES & QUOTES:
This book is probably best known for the story of Samson & Delilah, the cutting of Samson's hair and his subsequent loss of strength.

It is perhaps not so well known for the rape and murder of the Levites concubine, and the subsequent punishment of the tribe of Benjamin by the other tribes – which almost led to its complete annihilation.

Israel had reached an all-time low during this period, when they had backslidden massively from the will of The Lord. The lesson here is that disobedience will always bring mayhem and destruction, but repentance will bring about God's mercy always.

******

Ruth:

WHEN:
Thought to be written in the monarchic period around 100B.C.

WHO:
Generally ascribed to the Prophet Samuel.

PEOPLE & PLACES:
Ruth; Naomi; Boaz
Bethlehem; Moab

SOUND-BITES:
May the Lord reward your work, and your wages be full from the Lord, the God of Israel, under whose wings you have come to seek refuge." (Ch.2:12)

The neighbour women gave him a name, saying, "A son has been born to Naomi!" So they named him Obed. He is the father of Jesse, the father of David. (Ch.4:17)

THE MESSIANIC LINK:

Ruth is the great grandmother of King David (The line of Jesse) from whom comes Jesus.

Jesus is typified in Boaz the kinsman redeemer.

THE BOOK:

This is a short book of only 4 chapters that encompasses the aspect of redemption and love. Ruth and Orpah are widowed when their husbands die; after which Naomi (their mother-in-law) takes Ruth along with her back to Bethlehem. She is then taken care of by Boaz who eventually marries her and she bears him a son called Obed, whom her mother-in-law Naomi helps to take care off.

NOTES & QUOTES:

This is a book that encompasses the grim times during the period of Judges. It is a light in the midst of darkness in some way, and particularly poignant to Christians as Ruth becomes the great grandmother of King David. Here we have a book of love and loyalty, shown in the loyalty of Ruth towards Naomi and the love of Boaz towards Ruth. Boaz is a righteous man who 'does the right thing' by marrying Ruth and consequently bringing her into the lineage of Christ, thereby fulfilling the plans of God.

******

1 Samuel:

WHEN:
Around 930 B.C. Covering period of 1100-1000 B.C.

WHO:
Author anonymous, though traditionally ascribed to Samuel.

PEOPLE & PLACES:
Samuel; Hannah; Saul; David; Jonathan; Goliath; Nathan Israel; Ephraim; Shiloh; Ashdod; Gilgal; Bethlehem; Nob; Moab; Mount Gilboa

SOUND-BITES:
"For this boy I prayed, and the Lord has given me my petition which I asked of Him. **28**. So I have also dedicated him to the Lord; as long as he lives he is dedicated to the Lord." And he worshiped the Lord there. (Ch.1:27-28)

"But now your kingdom shall not endure. The Lord has sought out for Himself a man after His own heart, and the Lord has appointed him as ruler over His people, because you have not kept what the Lord commanded you." (Ch.13:14)

"..Behold, to obey is better than sacrifice,
And to heed than the fat of rams." (Ch.15:22)

THE MESSIANIC LINK:
Messiah exalted by God with power (1 Sam 2:10)
He would be a descendant of David (2 Sam 7:12-16)
The Rock of 2 Sam 23

Typified in the life of King David in exile (1 Sam:22)
Typified in the life of Jonathan the Faithful Friend (1 Sam 18)

THE BOOK:

The book of Samuel begins with the events leading up to the birth of Samuel, who would later become a righteous Judge over Israel. It continues with the people asking Samuel to anoint a King over them, as Samuels sons were not as wise as he was. It was a rejection of the era of the Judges and a yearning to be like the other nations. Samuel is not happy, but God assures him that it is His leadership and not Samuel's that the people are rejecting. (Ch.8)
Saul is appointed as King, and begins well but is soon at odds with The Lord, who displaces him with David a mere shepherd boy. (Ch.16:11-13)
The newly anointed David (not yet king) defeats Goliath in battle (Ch.17). He befriends king Saul's son Jonathan, but incurs the jealousy of Saul himself, who is tormented by an evil spirit and pursues David relentlessly.
The book of 1 Samuel ends with king Saul defeated by his enemies; Saul summoning the dead Samuel through the offices of the witch of En-dor (Ch.28) and being informed of his coming death, and that of his sons. (Ch.28:19)

NOTES & QUOTES:

This book is a story of lost opportunities; Saul had everything and yet he rebelled against God, thinking that he knew better (Ch.13:13-14). Consequently he lost everything – including his life and that of his sons in battle against their enemies.

Sometimes it is all too easy to lose patience whilst waiting on The Lord, and attempt to do things in our own strength thinking that we can 'hurry things along.' It is always a mistake to pre-empt The Lords plans!

******

2 Samuel:

WHEN:
Around 930 B.C. Covering period of 1100-1000 B.C.

WHO:
Author anonymous, though traditionally ascribed to Samuel.

PEOPLE & PLACES:
David; Bathsheba; Uriah; Nathan; Abner; Joab; Hiram; Absalom; Tamar

Ziklag; Mount Gilboa; Hebron; Judah; Jerusalem;

SOUND-BITES:
"Your house and your kingdom shall endure before Me forever; your throne shall be established forever." (Ch.7:16)

He said, "The Lord is my rock and my fortress and my deliverer; My God, my rock, in whom I take refuge,

My shield and the horn of my salvation, my stronghold and my refuge; My savior, You save me from violence. (Ch.22:2-3)

Then David said to Gad, "I am in great distress. Let us now fall into the hand of the Lord for His mercies are great, but do not let me fall into the hand of man." (Ch.24:14)

THE MESSIANIC LINK:

He would be a descendant of King David. (2 Sam.7:12-13)
He is the light of the morning. (2 Sam. 23:2-4)

THE BOOK:

The story starts with David mourning Saul and his sons, then moves on to stories of conquest and victory over their enemies. However things start to go bad when King David falls for Bathsheba, Uriah the Hittites wife; and arranges for the commanders death at the battle front. God forgives him, but warns trouble will begin in his own home.

Absalom kills Amnon for raping his half-sister Tamar, and goes into exile for a time. When he returns with David's permission; he leads a rebellion against David and sets himself up on the throne of David for a short while. Finally he is killed; against the wishes of King David.

The book ends with King David doing a census of the people against the wishes of God, and suffering the effects of a plague sent by The Lord to punish him. 70,000 people perish before the pestilence was held in check by King David offering sacrifice on a new alter on the threshing floor of Araunah the Jebusite.

NOTES & QUOTES:

I always find it somewhat incredible that King David who was a '*man after God's own heart*' should fall from grace as he does. However the lesson is that there is no-one who can afford to drop their guard, when it comes to following the will of God. I often say 'the devil is a busy man!' but it is the simple truth. Later in the new testament (1 Peter.5:8) the word tells us to '*Be of sober spirit, be on the alert. Your adversary, the devil, prowls around like a roaring lion, seeking someone to devour.*'

If Godly men such as King David and later Solomon can be 'got at' then we must truly all be on our guard against the wiles of Satan.

******

1 Kings:

WHEN:
Most likely between 561 and 538 B.C.

WHO:
Jewish tradition says Jeremiah, but evidence inconclusive.

PEOPLE & PLACES:
King David; King Solomon; Bathsheba; Hiram; Queen of Sheba; Rehoboam; Jeroboam; Elijah; Jezebel; Ahab; Jerusalem; Israel; Judah; Zarepath; Mount Carmel;

SOUND-BITES:

"As the Lord has been with my lord the king, so may He be with Solomon, and make his throne greater than the throne of my lord King David!" (Ch.1:37)

Now Solomon ruled over all the kingdoms from the River to the land of the Philistines and to the border of Egypt; they brought tribute and served Solomon all the days of his life. (Ch.4:21)

So King Solomon became greater than all the kings of the earth in riches and in wisdom.
24. All the earth was seeking the presence of Solomon, to hear his wisdom which God had put in his heart. (Ch.10:23,24)

Ahab the son of Omri did evil in the sight of the Lord more than all who were before him. (Ch.16:30)

THE MESSIANIC LINK:
Jesus is typified in the life of Solomon. The name *Solomon* means peace. Isaiah 9:6 describes the Messiah as the 'Prince of Peace.'

THE BOOK:

The book of Kings is a narrative history of the Kings of Israel and Judah. The first 2 chapters concentrate on events leading up to, and including, the death of King David in old age. He is succeeded by his son Solomon, who builds a reputation as a righteous judge and powerful monarch. The Lord himself – through Nathan the Prophet - gives him the name 'Jedediah' meaning beloved of the Lord. (2 Sam.12:25).

Upon King Solomon's death however the kingdom is split and divided between his son Rehoboam – who leads the southern kingdom of Judah; and his deposed commander Jeroboam – who leads the northern kingdom of Israel, and encourages them to worship other gods than Yahweh. There follows a succession of Kings both good and bad, the worst being Ahab, described as the most evil king Israel ever had. (Ch. 16:30)

Notes & Quotes:

In my mind this book emphasises just how important it is for a country or nation to have good leadership. As well as how easy it is for even very 'Godly' people to get involved in very 'ungodly' things. King Solomon seemingly had everything, including a deep and personal relationship with The Lord; and yet in his later days he backslid with the best of them and reduced his own people to slavery – hence the revolt and split when he died.

The story of the most evil King Ahab, who repented in his old age and was accepted by God; is a tremendous example of The Lords capacity to forgive no matter how bad the crime. (Ch.21:27-29)

******

2 Kings:

When:

Most likely between 561 and 538 B.C.

WHO:
Jewish tradition says Jeremiah, but evidence inconclusive.

PEOPLE & PLACES:
Elijah; Elisha; Isaiah; Hezekiah; Josiah; Nebuchadnezzar; Pharaoh Neco

Judah; Israel; Samaria; Moab; Aram; Babylon

SOUND-BITES:
When they had crossed over, Elijah said to Elisha, "Ask what I shall do for you before I am taken from you." And Elisha said, "Please, let a double portion of your spirit be upon me." (Ch.2:9)

So they poured *it* out for the men to eat. And as they were eating of the stew, they cried out and said, "O man of God, there is death in the pot." And they were unable to eat. (Ch.4:40)

So Hezekiah answered, "It is easy for the shadow to decline ten steps; no, but let the shadow turn backward ten steps." Isaiah the prophet cried to the Lord, and He brought the shadow on the stairway back ten steps by which it had gone down on the stairway of Ahaz. (Ch.20:10-11)

MESSIANIC LINK:
The Messiah is typified in the life and miracles of the Prophet Elisha.

THE BOOK:
2 Kings begins with the end ministry of the Prophet Elijah and his replacement with his student Elisha. Thereafter there is a running commentary of the Kings of Israel, who

were mostly bad; and the Kings of Judah who were mostly good but still bad at one time or another!

The prophet's Elijah, Elisha and Isaiah are a guiding light for the Kings, but even they cannot stop the decline into idolatry by both kingdoms.

It all leads to the capture of Samaria of the northern kingdom of Israel by the Assyrians (Ch.17); and the siege and capture of southern kingdom & Jerusalem by Nebuchadnezzar in chapter 25.

NOTES & QUOTES:

The history of Israel and Judah – the divided kingdom of David; shows that God is a God of many chances – but he is also a God of the last chance! There comes a point where He will exact justice or retribution for sins committed; especially where there is no repentance offered.

The Kings and Peoples of both kingdoms repeatedly resorted to idolatry, and abandoned their God Yahweh. This led ultimately to the loss of Israel in its entirety and the deportation of Judah into Babylon.

"You shall have no other gods before Me." (Ex.20:3)

******

1 Chronicles:

WHEN:
Around 400 B.C.

WHO:

Traditionally written by Ezra.

PEOPLE & PLACES:
King David; Twelve tribes
Israel; Judah; Jerusalem

SOUND-BITES:
So all the elders of Israel came to the king at Hebron, and David made a covenant with them in Hebron before the Lord; and they anointed David king over Israel, according to the word of the Lord through Samuel. (Ch.11:3)

It happened when the ark of the covenant of the Lord came to the city of David, that Michal the daughter of Saul looked out of the window and saw King David leaping and celebrating; and she despised him in her heart. (Ch.15:29)

Yours, O Lord, is the greatness and the power and the glory and the victory and the majesty, indeed everything that is in the heavens and the earth; Yours is the dominion, O Lord, and You exalt Yourself as head over all. (Ch.29:11)

THE MESSIANIC LINK:
Messiah would come from the tribe of Judah (1 Chron 5:2, Luke 3:23-32)

THE BOOK:
The book of Chronicles begins with a genealogy of the tribes of Israel and the house of David, covering in some extra detail, most of the information already covered by 1 & 2 Samuel and 1 & 2 Kings.

By chapter 10 most of the genealogies have gone, to be replaced with more detail regarding the defeat and death of Saul and the Reign of King David.

David is inspired by the devil to take a census of the people, (Ch.21) thus incurring the wrath of God and losing 70,000 men to pestilence.

The book ends with the death of King David and the beginning of the rule of his son Solomon.

NOTES & QUOTES:

This book fills in the 'gaps' regarding the genealogy and history of the Israelites. The main lessons to be found here are that God is faithful and (Ch.11:1-3) and that disobedience brings judgement as sure as obedience brings blessing.

******

2 Chronicles:

WHEN:
Around 400 B.C.

WHO:
Traditionally written by Ezra.

PEOPLE & PLACES:
King David; King Solomon; Rehoboam: Jeroboam; Nebuchadnezzar
Judah; Israel; Jerusalem; Mount Moriah; Persia

SOUND-BITES:

Now Solomon the son of David established himself securely over his kingdom, and the Lord his God was with him and exalted him greatly. (Ch.1:1)

When all Israel *saw* that the king did not listen to them the people answered the king, saying,
"What portion do we have in David?
We have no inheritance in the son of Jesse.
Every man to your tents, O Israel;
Now look after your own house, David." Ch.10:16)

THE MESSIANIC LINK:

Typified in Solomon's temple, and in the greatness and wisdom of Solomon.

THE BOOK:

This book is mainly concerned with the southern kingdom of Judah, and only mentions Israel when the two 'collide' so to speak. Taken from a Priestly point of view it tends to concentrate on the spiritual well-being or otherwise of Judah.
In chapter's 2-7 Solomon builds and dedicates the Temple. There-after the rules of the different Kings are gone into in more detail, as is the destruction of both the Northern and the Southern kingdoms.
The book ends with the return from exile in Babylon, of the Southern kingdom of Judah.

NOTES & QUOTES:

It is well noted that only the southern kingdom of Judah, actually returned back home again, after the fall of Babylon to the Persian King Cyrus the Great. This is because The Lord made sure that his people in captivity would still retain their identity, thereby ensuring the lineage through which the Messiah would come.

Israel, the idolatrous Northern Kingdom was however scattered throughout the lands of the Assyrians, never to be found again.

******

Ezra:

WHEN:
Not certain, but around 450 B.C.

WHO:
Generally considered to be Ezra and Nehemiah.

PEOPLE & PLACES:
Cyrus: Ezra; Nebuchadnezzar; Artaxerxes; Darius
Judah; Jerusalem;

SOUND-BITES:
They sang, praising and giving thanks to the Lord, saying, "For He is good, for His lovingkindness is upon Israel forever." And all the people shouted with a great shout when they praised the Lord because the foundation of the house of the Lord was laid. (Ch.3:11)

This Ezra went up from Babylon, and he was a scribe skilled in the law of Moses, which the Lord God of Israel had given; and the king granted him all he requested because the hand of the Lord his God was upon him. (Ch.7:6)

"…Thus I was strengthened according to the hand of the Lord my God upon me, and I gathered leading men from Israel to go up with me." (Ch.7:28)

THE MESSIANIC LINK:

Messiah typified in Zerubbabel who rebuilt the Temple.

THE BOOK:

This is a period that covers the return of the Judean exiles to their homeland by decree of Cyrus. The return takes place over three time periods, firstly under Zerubbabel we have the reconstruction of the Temple (Ch.1-6). Then Ezra re-unites the community (Ch.7-10) finally Nehemiah sees to the building of the walls surrounding the city of Jerusalem. This book is concerned with the first two phases of the return, the theme of the book is Restoration in both a physical and spiritual sense.

NOTES & QUOTES:

The return from exile in Babylon did not happen all at once owing to several factors, not the least of which being that the Jews had made a life for themselves during the long period of captivity in Babylon; and some were there-fore reluctant to return. After 70 years had passed, most of the people had no memory of Jerusalem at all, being born in

Babylon where they had set up a community and the institution of the Synagogue.

******

Nehemiah:

WHEN:
Not certain, but around 450 B.C.

WHO:
Generally considered to be Ezra and Nehemiah.

PEOPLE & PLACES:
Ezra; Artaxerxes; Nehemiah
Judah; Jerusalem; Persia

SOUND-BITES:
They said to me, "The remnant there in the province who survived the captivity are in great distress and reproach, and the wall of Jerusalem is broken down and its gates are burned with fire."
When I heard these words, I sat down and wept and mourned for days.. (Ch1:3-4)

So we built the wall and the whole wall was joined together to half its height, for the people had a mind to work. (Ch.4:6)

So the wall was completed on the twenty-fifth of the month Elul, in fifty-two days. When all our enemies heard of it, and all the nations surrounding us saw it, they lost their confidence; for they recognized that this work had been accomplished with the help of our God. (Ch.6:15-16)

THE MESSIANIC LINK:

The Messiah is typified in the person and ministry of Nehemiah – the re-builder of the walls.

THE BOOK:

Nehemiah begins where Ezra left off, with the continuation of the return, and (for his part) the re-building of the walls of Jerusalem; after a plea from the inhabitants. Nehemiah manages to counter the plots by the locals to prevent building, and instead completes the walls in only 52 days (Ch.6:15).

Chapter 8 sees the feast of booths restored, and a return to true worship as the people confess their sins (Ch.9) and gather together to sign a new Covenant with the Lord (Ch.10), as Nehemiah sets up a round of reforms designed to bring the people into line.

NOTES & QUOTES:

Nehemiah was not only a deeply spiritual man, but he was also a realist; just the sort of man The Lord needed at that time to bring the people back to true worship. Nehemiah prayed for success and protection whilst he was building – but also seen to it that the builders were protected by armed guards! Its called Faith in Action. (Ch.4:9)

Hard work coupled by prayer, is a potent weapon against the wiles of the enemy who would seek to discourage and destroy us, or our efforts to worship the Lord. Prayer first –

to seek God's will - then hard graft to complete his wishes; is a potent force no matter what the circumstance.

******

Esther:

WHEN:
No definite date but likely between 450-350 B.C.

WHO:
Traditionally Mordecai

PEOPLE & PLACES:
Esther; Mordecai; Haman; Ahasuerus
India; Ethiopia;

SOUND-BITES:
The king loved Esther more than all the women, and she found favor and kindness with him more than all the virgins, so that he set the royal crown on her head and made her queen instead of Vashti. (Ch.2:17)

For if you remain silent at this time, relief and deliverance will arise for the Jews from another place and you and your father's house will perish. And who knows whether you have not attained royalty for such a time as this?" (Ch.4:14)

Then Queen Esther replied, "If I have found favor in your sight, O king, and if it pleases the king, let my life be given me as my petition, and my people as my request;" (Ch.7:3)

THE MESSIANIC LINK:

Messiah typified in the person of Mordecai.

THE BOOK:

The book of Esther begins with the all-powerful King of Persia (Ahasuerus), banishing his Queen and seeking a replacement. Esther - the adopted daughter of Mordecai - finds favor with the King and is accepted as Queen of the realm (Ch.2:17). Her position is further strengthened when Mordecai uncovers a plot against the King, and informs him through Esther.

Chapter 3 sees Haman plotting to have the Jews eliminated, and results in Esther successfully petitioning the King to have it stopped, after Mordecai reminds her of her duty (Ch.4:8-14).

She is successful and Haman is hanged on the very gallows that he had prepared for the Jews; who are also given the chance of revenge against their enemies.

NOTES & QUOTES:

Even though The Lord God is mentioned nowhere in this book, his presence is implied throughout. In Esther we have an example of the importance of 'kinship,' and how God would at times place individuals in places of power and influence in order to fulfill his plans.

Even though Esther could have saved her own life here by keeping quiet, she chose to risk her life by appealing to the King for mercy; as the penalty for disturbing the King was death.

Greater love has no one than this, that one lay down his life for his friends. (John.15:13)

******

Job:

WHEN:
Impossible to say; but generally thought to be the oldest book in the Bible.

WHO:
No clear author is mentioned, and no clue given.

PEOPLE & PLACES:
Job; Eliphaz; Bildad; Zophar; Elihu;
The land of Uz

SOUND-BITES:
The Lord said to Satan, "From where do you come?" Then Satan answered the Lord and said, "From roaming about on the earth and walking around on it." (Ch.1:7)

Then Job arose and tore his robe and shaved his head, and he fell to the ground and worshiped. He said,
"Naked I came from my mother's womb,
And naked I shall return there.
The Lord gave and the Lord has taken away.
Blessed be the name of the Lord." (Ch.1:20-21)

Then the Lord answered Job out of the whirlwind and said, "Who is this that darkens counsel By words without knowledge? (Ch.38:1-2)

THE MESSIANIC LINK:

Messiah typified in the sufferings and eventual blessings of Job.

THE BOOK:

The story of Job begins with a man who has everything. Health, wealth, respect, and a healthy family, as well as a love for God. Satan challenges the Lord regarding Jobs love, and says it will soon fade away if God removes the blessings that he has given him.

Job's sufferings begin as he loses everything that he has to some tragedy or other – including his family. In chapter 2 satan is given permission to take away his health also, and he is smote with boils and sores.

Thereafter we have a dialogue between Job and his friends, as they try to determine why this has happened. The consensus of opinion between Jobs friends is that he has some unconfessed sin, as they maintain the God does not punish the innocent (Ch.4).

Finally God speaks in chapter 38 and rebukes them all for their lack of understanding.

Job repents in dust and ashes (Ch.42), and his fortunes are restored two-fold.

NOTES & QUOTES:

The book of Job teaches us that misfortune and calamity can happen to anyone, and that it is not an indication of The Lords ill will towards us! Job is described as Righteous, and yet Satan is allowed to torment and punish him to try and break his love for The Lord – he did not succeed. Job did however become very frustrated with his lot, and who can blame him!

One important point here is that Satan can only operate under God's permissive will.

******

Psalms

WHEN:
Written throughout the period of Israel's History, most probably put together after he return from Babylon around 537 B.C.

WHO:
King David; King Solomon; Moses; Asaph; The sons of Korah; Heman; Ethan the Ezrahite

PEOPLE & PLACES:
King David; King Solomon
Jerusalem; Judah; Israel; Egypt

SOUND BITES:
How blessed is the man who does not walk in the counsel of the wicked, nor stand in the path of sinners, nor sit in the seat of scoffers!
But his delight is in the law of the Lord, and in His law he meditates day and night. (Ch.1:1-2)

The heavens are telling of the glory of God;
and their expanse is declaring the work of His hands. (Ch.19:1)

For dogs have surrounded me;

A band of evildoers has encompassed me;

They pierced my hands and my feet.

17. I can count all my bones.

They look, they stare at me;

18. They divide my garments among them,

And for my clothing they cast lots. (Ch.22:16-18)

Create in me a clean heart, O God,

And renew a steadfast spirit within me. (Ch.51:10)

THE MESSIANIC LINK:

Messiah would be the Son of God (Ps 2:7, 12,)

Messiah would not be abandoned to death. (Ps 16:8-10,)

Messiah would be scorned & crucified (Ps 22:6-8)

Messiah would be unjustly hated (Ps 69:4,)

Messiah would be Lord, seated at the right hand of God (Ps 110:1,5,)

In the line of Melchizedek (Ps 110:4,)

Messiah would be rejected 'stone' (Ps 118:22)

Other Messianic Psalms: Chapters 2, 8, 16, 22, 45, 69, 89, 109, 110, 118

THE BOOK:

This book gets its name from the Greek, "a song sung to the accompaniment of a musical instrument." Fundamentally it is aimed at praise and worship, however it also covers many aspects of human existence such as tragedy, war, wisdom, love, justice, fear and lamentation.

Prophecies and verses relating to the coming Messiah are peppered throughout the book – as seen in the previous

'Messianic Links'- and a large part of it describes the trials & sufferings of David as he runs from a vengeful Saul; indeed King David is listed as author in 73 different occasions.

Psalm 22 is perhaps one of the most powerful, as it describes the suffering of the messiah on the cross in great detail – an example of prophecy in the psalms that was fulfilled in full with the crucified Christ.

NOTES & QUOTES:

Although this book is generally not regarded as a theological work, it nevertheless plays a major role in our understanding of God and his dealings with us. It teaches us and comforts us in equal measures, thanks to the vast range of subjects that are discussed throughout.

The influence of the book of Psalms continues to play an important part in the praise and worship that we enjoy today, as well as enabling us to enjoy The Lords presence even in the most troublesome of circumstances; through the reading of this powerful work.

There is a Psalm for every occasion it seems, whether you are in a situation that calls for celebration, lamentation or simple reflection; the book of Psalms has it all.

******

Proverbs:

WHEN:

Around 900 B.C. During the reign of King Solomon.

WHO:
Mostly ascribed to Solomon (Ch.1:1).

PEOPLE & PLACES:
King Solomon; Agur; Lemuel
Israel

SOUND-BITES:
The fear of the Lord is the beginning of knowledge;
Fools despise wisdom and instruction. (Ch.1:7)

"The beginning of wisdom is: Acquire wisdom;
And with all your acquiring, get understanding." (Ch.4:7)

For the lips of an adulteress drip honey
And smoother than oil is her speech; (Ch.5:3)

A wise son makes a father glad,
But a foolish son is a grief to his mother. (Ch.10:1)

He who mocks the poor taunts his Maker;
He who rejoices at calamity will not go unpunished.
(Ch.17:5)

THE MESSIANIC LINK:
Messiah was established from the beginning (Ch.8:22-23)
He would be the Son of God. (Ch.30:4)
He is typified in the writings about wisdom.

THE BOOK:
The agenda or theme of Proverbs is written out in the first
chapter versus 1-6. and is basically a book primarily
devoted to giving out wisdom and wise instruction to the
reader.

Solomon was well known and respected for his wisdom in dealing with difficult matters, and Kings, dignitaries and learned people would travel for miles to hear his sound advice.

Wisdom itself plays the biggest role throughout the book, as it is linked to knowing God, prosperity and long life. Wisdom itself is promoted right from the first chapter as beginning with 'the fear of The Lord' (Ch.1:7)

NOTES & QUOTES:

Proverbs is one of the books of the Bible that is ideally suited to reading a chapter or two per day, as it is not a book that follows long story lines.

The wisdom of Solomon just pours out of every verse and chapter; and even though written some 3,000 years ago, still carries the same impact now as it did then.

There is a recurring theme through-out this book, and that is to 'be smart.' Trust in God and acquire wisdom from Him, so that you may "Live long and prosper" to coin a modern-day phrase!

******

Ecclesiastes:

WHEN:
Approx 925 B.C.

WHO:
Traditionally ascribed to King Solomon.

People & Places:
The Preacher
Jerusalem

Sound-Bites:
And I set my mind to know wisdom and to know madness and folly; I realized that this also is striving after wind. Because in much wisdom there is much grief, and increasing knowledge results in increasing pain. (Ch.1:17-18)

There is an appointed time for everything. And there is a time for every event under heaven. (Ch.3:1)
He who loves money will not be satisfied with money, nor he who loves abundance with its income. This too is vanity. (Ch.5:10)

The Messianic Link:
Messiah is typified in the wisdom of God, for without Him, then life is utterly meaningless.

The Book:
Ecclesiastes is so depressing on the face of it, that many have wondered why it is even included in the canon of scripture! The fact is however this is a work by the 'Preacher' that explores every aspect of life as it presents itself, and removes the concept or influence of God.
His conclusion is that life without the presence of God at its foundation is utterly meaningless and a *striving after the wind* (Ch.1:14)

He finishes this work by encouraging people to *'fear God and keep his commandments'* that all may be well with them.

NOTES & THOUGHTS:

'There is nothing new under the sun' is perhaps a quote that is known by many, but few people know that it is straight from the Bible! (Ch.1:1) Ecclesiastes is a treasure trove of wisdom in the same way as is Proverbs or Psalms, it just seems to come out all a bit depressing!

A good tip when reading this book, is always to keep in mind that the Preacher is talking about life without divine purpose or influence – a meaningless life that could have no worthwhile conclusion – a bit like atheism!

******

The Song of Solomon:

WHEN:
Around 945 B.C

WHO:
Traditionally ascribed to Solomon.

PEOPLE & PLACES:
Solomon; Shulammite bride.
Jerusalem

SOUND-BITES:
"I am the rose of Sharon,
The lily of the valleys." (Ch.2:1)

"Your lips, my bride, drip honey;
Honey and milk are under your tongue,
And the fragrance of your garments is like the fragrance of
Lebanon. (Ch.4:11)

THE MESSIANIC LINK:
The Messiah is typified in the bridegrooms love and
marriage to the bride (The Church).

He is The Rose of Sharon, and the Lily of the valley
(Ch.2:1)

THE BOOK:
This is a book filled with the expressions of love between a
man and a woman – namely King Solomon and the
Shulammite bride.
The book follows the courting of the young couple, and as
such is divided into three parts; the courtship itself, the
wedding and the actual marriage.
The union of a man and woman are celebrated here as an
expression of what God intended for his creation, and as
such counters the extremes of asceticism (the denial of
pleasure), and hedonism (pleasure above all things).

NOTES & QUOTES:
Whoever thinks that a Christian cannot enjoy sex, should
perhaps take another look at the Song of Solomon!
The love expressions, and marriage of King Solomon to the
Shulammite bride is the example God gives us as his
perfect will regarding our relationship with our wives; and
this very much includes passion, as well as care and delight
in our marriage partners.

Allegorically, there is also the parallelism between Christ and his Bride (the Church) alluded to, in the relationship between the Shulammite bride and King Solomon.

******

Isaiah:

WHEN:
700 - 680 B.C.

WHO:
Isaiah the Prophet (Ch.1:1)

PEOPLE & PLACES:
Isaiah; Hezekiah; Cyrus
Judah; Jerusalem; Israel; Moab; Philistia; Assyria; Babylon

SOUND-BITES:
"Come now, and let us reason together," Says the Lord, "Though your sins are as scarlet, They will be as white as snow; Though they are red like crimson, They will be like wool. (Ch.1:18)

For a child will be born to us, a son will be given to us; And the government will rest on His shoulders; (Ch.9:6)

But He was pierced through for our transgressions, He was crushed for our iniquities; The chastening for our well-being fell upon Him, And by His scourging we are healed. (Ch.53:5)

THE MESSIANIC LINK:

The Messiah is typified in the 'Suffering Servant' passages.
He is born of a virgin (Ch.7:14)
He would be God and man. (Ch.9:6)
Messiah would heal the sick. (Ch.35:5-6)
He would be rejected by the Jews. (Ch.49:7)
He would be whipped and scourged. (Ch.50:6)
Messiah would be the perfect sacrifice. (Ch.53)

THE BOOK:

Isaiah the Prophet spoke mainly to the people of Judah and the message was mostly to 'repent' and turn from their wicked ways that the Lord might bless them yet again. God has tried to reason with them, but they are a 'stubborn people' Isaiah gets his commission in chapter 6 when God asks whom he will send; and Isaiah volunteers (Ch.6:8). Isaiah is particularly concerned or focused on the coming of the Messiah, a savior who will also be a 'light unto the nations' (Ch.42:6).

Throughout this book, Isaiah rages against hypocrisy and the double-dealings of those who would claim to be 'religious' and God-fearing; warning that the Judgment of God is about to descend upon them with a 'consuming fire' (Ch.30:30,33) unless they repent from their ways.

NOTES & QUOTES:

It's fair to say I think that the Prophet Isaiah is one of the 'giants' amongst the Bible Prophets. In today's world he would probably have his own TV show! In fact even in his own day, he was a man widely recognized as being a force to be reckoned with and a definite 'conduit' between man and his Creator; when he spoke, people listened.

One of the main themes throughout this book apart from repentance, is the prophecies concerning the coming Messiah. From his lowly birth (Chs.7,9) to the fact that he would suffer an ignominious death on a cross (Ch.53), thus making himself the perfect sacrifice for mankind's sins; it is all written in graphic detail throughout the book of Isaiah.

******

Jeremiah:

WHEN:
Most likely written during the time of exile 587–538 B.C.

WHO:
Jeremiah the Prophet.

PEOPLE & PLACES:
Jeremiah; Nebuchadnezzar; Zedekiah; Pharaoh
Judah; Jerusalem; Babylon; Ammon; Damascus

SOUND-BITES:
"Before I formed you in the womb I knew you,
And before you were born I consecrated you;
I have appointed you a prophet to the nations." (Ch.1:5)

"The heart is more deceitful than all else; And is desperately sick; Who can understand it? (Ch.17:9)

For I know the plans that I have for you,' declares the Lord, 'plans for welfare and not for calamity to give you a future and a hope. (Ch.29:11)

THE MESSIANIC LINK:

Messiah is the 'righteous branch' our Righteousness. (Ch.23:5)
He is The Lord Almighty (Ch.23:6)

THE BOOK:

Jeremiah pronounces the coming Judgment of God throughout this book, earning him the name of 'the weeping prophet' amongst many scholars.
Judah had fallen far from the will of God, and had sunk into idolatry and immorality; Jeremiah even describing Judah as a 'harlot' in chapter 22:20.
Even with Jeremiah weeping in their ears however, they did not repent, but instead threw him into a cistern (Ch.32) to shut him up.
The final chapters see the fulfillment of Jeremiah's prophecy's regarding their Judgment, as Nebuchadnezzar arrives to destroy Jerusalem and take the people into captivity.

NOTES & QUOTES:

Bad news is seldom welcomed, that's a fact. However Jeremiah preached not only the bad news, he also preached the way to prevent it from coming to pass – repentance.
The people though could only hear the prophet telling them what they could NOT do, and chose to ignore the

alternatives; so they threw him into an old cistern thinking that would be the end of it.

God however will not be mocked (Gal.6:7), and his Judgment's will come to pass. Even though sometimes it looks like nothing is happening, we have to remember that it is in His time – not ours!

******

Lamentations:

WHEN:
Most likely written during the time of exile 587–538 B.C.

WHO:
Jeremiah the Prophet.

PEOPLE & PLACES:
Jeremiah
Judah; Jerusalem; Israel

SOUND-BITES:
How lonely sits the city
That was full of people!
She has become like a widow
Who was once great among the nations!
She who was a princess among the provinces
Has become a forced laborer! (Ch.1:1)

Restore us to You, O Lord, that we may be restored;
Renew our days as of old, (Ch.5:21)

The Messianic Link:

The Messiah is captive (Ch.4:20)
See Jeremiah.

The Book:

Lamentations really carries on where Jeremiah left of, and continues to mourn the loss of Jerusalem and the extent of the punishment that the Lord has put upon them. Jerusalem is laid waste, it's people either captured or killed. In chapter 4 we see the depths of depravation that the siege had brought them to, as it reduced them to the cannibalization of their own children.

Notes & Quotes:

Lamentations is full of mourning for the people of Judah and the city of Jerusalem. The fact is however that the people repented after the event; a bit like saying you're sorry only because you have been caught! Throughout the book of Jeremiah, the Prophet warned them what was to come if they did not turn from their wicked ways; and in Lamentations we have the inevitable result when they refused.

As mentioned elsewhere; God is the God of many chances – he is also the God of the last chance!

******

Ezekiel:

When:

Between 593 and 571 B.C.

WHO:
Ezekiel the Prophet (Ch.1:3)

PEOPLE & PLACES:
Ezekiel; Pharaoh; Nebuchadnezzar
Judah; Jerusalem; Israel; Babylon; Moab; Edom; Tyre;
Egypt

SOUND-BITES:
Then He said to me, "Son of man, stand on your feet that I
may speak with you!" (Ch.2:1)

However, if you have warned the righteous man that the
righteous should not sin and he does not sin, he shall surely
live because he took warning; and you have delivered
yourself." (Ch.3:21)
So I prophesied as He commanded me, and the breath came
into them, and they came to life and stood on their feet, an
exceedingly great army. (Ch.37:10)

I will put My Spirit within you and you will come to life,
and I will place you on your own land. Then you will know
that I, the Lord, have spoken and done it," declares the
Lord.'" (Ch.37:14)

THE MESSIANIC LINK:
He is the 'Good Shepherd' in Ch.34:23

THE BOOK:
Ezekiel begins with Judgment on the house of Israel, and
particularly on the leaders of the nation who have been

lording it over the common people (Ch.34:1-6). Idolatrous elders are condemned (Ch:14), and Babylon is mentioned as the instrument of God's Judgment (Ch.21:21). The book is full of symbolism and allegory as Ezekiel is given visions of the future that include desolation and dispersion to Babylon. The surrounding nations are also to be Judged for rejoicing at Jerusalem's destruction (Chaps:25-32). Ezekiel finishes with hope of a final restoration of Israel as The Lord gives him a vision of *'the valley of dry bones'* (Ch.37).

NOTES & QUOTES:

Ezekiel was indeed the 'man of the moment' as God placed him amongst the exiles to show that He was not only God in geographical Judah; but that he was indeed God over all the Earth. It was a revelation to the people that they could still worship God, even without the Temple in Jerusalem itself. The Lord made that clear indeed, when he instigated the ministry of Ezekiel after he was led into exile with the rest of them.

The institution that we now know as the Synagogue began in Babylon, and this played a huge part in keeping the nation together whilst they were in captivity.

Sometimes just when everything seems lost, The Lord will indeed show us a way forward.

******

Daniel:

WHEN:
Around 530 B.C.

WHO:
Traditionally attributed to the Prophet Daniel.

PEOPLE & PLACES:
Daniel (Belteshaz-zar); Hananiah; Mishael; Azariah;
Nebuchadnezzar; Darius; Gabriel.
Judah; Jerusalem; Babylon; Persia

SOUND-BITES:
As for these four youths, God gave them knowledge and
intelligence in every branch of literature and wisdom;
Daniel even understood all kinds of visions and dreams.
(Ch.1:17)

As for every matter of wisdom and understanding about
which the king consulted them, he found them ten times
better than all the magicians and conjurers who were in all
his realm. (Ch.1:20)

The king answered Daniel and said, "Surely your God is a
God of gods and a Lord of kings and a revealer of
mysteries, since you have been able to reveal this mystery."
(Ch.2:47)

".....For He is the living God and enduring forever,
And His kingdom is one which will not be destroyed,
And His dominion will be forever." (Ch.6:26)

THE MESSIANIC LINK:

Messiah is the 'Son of Man' (Ch.7:13-14)
He is the Stone that smashes the kingdoms, and the
everlasting kingdom. (Ch.2:34,44)
He is the fourth man in the fiery furnace. (Ch.3:25)

THE BOOK:

This book follows the visions and ministry of Daniel after
he has been deported to Babylon by Nebuchadnezzar. The
first chapter begins with the appointment of Daniel and his
three friends Hananiah, Mishael and Azariah; into the royal
court of Nebuchadnezzar and taken on as 'wise men' or
advisors to the King.

In the second chapter Daniel interprets a disturbing dream
that Nebuchadnezzar has, thereby leading to the promotion
of Daniel to Chief Prefect. Chapter 3 however sees Daniel's
three friends (re-named Shadrach, Meshach & Abed-nego)
thrown into a furnace for their refusal to worship the golden
statue – only to be saved by God and the 'fourth man' in
the furnace with them.

King Nebuchadnezzar acknowledges 'Daniel's God' in
chapter 4, and goes mad for 7 years according to the Word
spoke by Daniel. Chapter 5 sees Nebuchadnezzar's son
Belshazzar and the passage relating to the writing on the
wall that Daniel interprets correctly to prophesy the end of
the Belshazzar's kingdom.

In Chapter 6 Daniel is thrown into the lion's den by his new
ruler Darius the Mede, but God closes the mouths of the
lion's and he is unscathed, and promoted by King Darius.

The last chapters are all prophecies and visions relating to the 'end times' and in particular the time of 'Tribulation' a period of seven years of turmoil to come in the last days. (Ch.9:24-27)

NOTES & QUOTES:

This is a complex, and at the same time exciting book. We have Daniel and his friends appointed as leaders over a nation that enslaved them. The escape from the fiery furnace and the escape from the lion's den; perhaps the most well-known of the stories, as well as Nebuchadnezzar's 7 yearlong madness!

This is also a most popular book for the students of eschatology (Studies relating to the end-times), and rightly so as the last 5 chapters are dedicated to the 'End Days' and full of allegory and visual stimuli as to just when it will all occur, and what we can expect to happen.

Along with the book of Revelation in the New Testament, this is a major book for anyone interested in the tribulation period, and just exactly where the Christians will be when it is happening!

Are you pre, mid, or post tribulation? That is the question!

******

Hosea:

Hosea is the first book of a series of short works we know as 'The Minor Prophets' owing to the fact that they are

short writings, and definitely not a slur on the importance of the books themselves – which is beyond any doubt.
For a more detailed yet compact study of these 12 Prophets, please refer to my ebook;

'Spotlight On The Minor Prophets.'

For sale through Amazon.

WHEN:
Written around 750-725 B.C.

WHO:
Hosea himself was the author (Ch.1:1)

PEOPLE & PLACES:
Hosea; Gomer
Israel; Judah; Assyria; Egypt;

SOUND-BITES:
Yet the number of the sons of Israel
Will be like the sand of the sea,
Which cannot be measured or numbered; (Ch.1:10)

"I will sow her for Myself in the land.
I will also have compassion on her who had not obtained compassion,
And I will say to those who were not My people,
'You are My people!'
And they will say, 'You are my God!'" (Ch.2:23)

Return, O Israel, to the Lord your God,
For you have stumbled because of your iniquity. (Ch.14:1)

THE MESSIANIC LINK:

The Messiah is typified in the faithfulness of Hosea – the loving husband.

THE BOOK:

Hosea (meaning *Salvation*) is a Prophet who was ministering around the 750 B.C. a time of great backsliding for the nation of Israel and Judah. Hosea sought to bring the people back to their God, and away from the idolatry that had consumed them.

Hosea can basically be split into two parts. 1st part; chapters 1-3: 2nd part; chapters 4-14.

This is a book rich in allegory and visual aids, where Hosea is instructed to marry a harlot, to whom he has 3 children; each of them have names that suggest 'unloved' or 'not wanted'.

This is how God sees them; they have 'played the field' with other gods and abandoned their first love. They have been faithless while God has been faithful to them.

Chapter 4 onwards describes in graphic detail the punishment that awaits them at the hands of an angry God unless they turn from their wicked ways.

NOTES & QUOTES:

The book of Hosea is all about relationship. A relationship that God desires to have with his people, and a relationship that demands respect and faithfulness.

The Lord was angry with the Israelites why? Because they were committing adultery!

They had broken the marriage covenant and God was determined to bring them back into relationship. Hosea 2:16. "It will come about in that day," declares the LORD THAT you will call Me Ishi, and will no longer call Me Baali.
(Ishi = "My Husband" , Baali = "My Master") Jeremiah 3:20
This is also a book about restoration, the willingness of God to forgive and forget...
" I will heal their apostasy, I will love them freely, For My anger has turned away from them." (Ch.14:4)

******

Joel:

WHEN:
Around 830-800 B.C.

WHO:
Joel the son of Pethuel (Ch.1:1)

PEOPLE & PLACES:
Joel
Judah; Jerusalem

SOUND-BITES:
What the gnawing locust has left, the swarming locust has eaten;
And what the swarming locust has left, the creeping locust has eaten;

And what the creeping locust has left, the stripping locust
has eaten. (Ch.1:4)

It will come about after this
That I will pour out My Spirit on all mankind;
And your sons and daughters will prophesy,
Your old men will dream dreams,
Your young men will see visions. (Ch2:28)

THE MESSIANIC LINK:
The Messiah is the savior of all mankind. (Ch2:32-28) and
the baptizer in the Holy Spirit. ((Ch.2:28-32)

THE BOOK:
Joel (meaning *The Lord is God*) wrote this book after a
terrible plague of Locust had ravaged the country; a plague
which was a warning of much worse to come if the people
of Judah did not repent. It is a book that is focused on the
'Great and terrible day of The Lord.' He tells the people
they must 'rend their hearts, and not their garments'
(Ch.2:13), in other words they must repent from the heart
and not just show the outward signs of repentance.
If this is done then God promises to forgive and restore
(Ch2:18 onwards); to judge the nations and to bless Judah.

NOTES & QUOTES:
Although this is a very short book, it is none the less a
powerful word. The main theme 'The Day of The Lord' is
tempered with the fact that there is still time for repentance
v32- 'whoever calls upon the name of the Lord will be
saved' again, a familiar scripture. Used by Paul in Romans
10:13.

Also 3:14 – even the valley of judgment is called the valley of decision!

Further proof that God is indeed 'slow to anger and abounding in loving-kindness' (2:13).

******

Amos:

WHEN:
Most likely written between 760-750 B.C.

WHO:
The Prophet Amos himself. (Ch.1:1)

PEOPLE & PLACES:
Amos; Jeroboam
Israel; Judah; Samaria;

SOUND-BITES:
Thus says the Lord,
"For three transgressions of Judah and for four
I will not revoke its punishment,
Because they rejected the law of the Lord
And have not kept His statutes; (Ch.2:4)

Surely the Lord God does nothing
Unless He reveals His secret counsel
To His servants the prophets. (Ch.3:7)

Then Amos replied to Amaziah, "I am not a prophet, nor am I the son of a prophet; for I am a herdsman and a grower of sycamore figs." (Ch.7:14)

"I will also plant them on their land,
And they will not again be rooted out from their land
Which I have given them,"
Says the Lord your God. (Ch.9:15)

THE MESSIANIC LINK:
God would darken the day at noon during Messiah's death (Amos 8:9, Matt 27:45-46)

THE BOOK:
The book of Amos (meaning *Burden Bearer*) follows a recurring theme of coming judgment.
 The first two chapters include eight condemnations introduced by the words " For three transgressions and for four" What's that all about ?
This was to empathise that the Lord was entitled to judge Israel on the basis of not just three transgressions; but four. This pointed to the severity of the crime and the coming judgment.
As with Hosea, Amos preached against the social and moral decline of Israel. The worship of Assyrian deities and the huge gulf that had emerged between the 'haves' and the 'have not's '
Assyria and Damascus had been at one another's throats for some years now and so Israel was 'allowed' to prosper in a material sense. They had winter houses and summer

houses, houses of Ivory (Amos 3:15). Houses of 'hewn stone' (5:11) and they reclined on "Beds of Ivory" (6:4)
They were "at ease in Zion" (6:1)
As in the book of Hosea "Religion" was prospering but Faith in the one true God YHWH was on the decline.
The book ends on a positive note however with the promise of glorious future for Israel (Ch.9:11-15).

NOTES & QUOTES:

Amos teaches us that material prosperity, while in itself not a bad thing, can nevertheless lead us away from God.
In effect the 'provision' takes the place of honor, while the 'provider' is forgotten about.
Faith is overshadowed by the 'appearance of religion,' and the social divisions are allowed to get out of control.
Another strong lesson to take from Amos is the fact that God used him – a mere shepherd (Ch.1:1), to act as his spokesman to his people. The phrase 'I'm only' does not exist in Gods list of good excuses! We may all be called upon at different times to answer the call of The Almighty, no matter how unimportant we think we are.

******

Obadiah:

WHEN:
Between 850-840 B.C.

WHO:

The Prophet Obadiah (vs.1)

PEOPLE & PLACES:
Obadiah
Edom; Jerusalem

SOUND-BITES:
"Do not gloat over your brother's day,
The day of his misfortune.
And do not rejoice over the sons of Judah
In the day of their destruction;
Yes, do not boast
In the day of their distress. (Ch.1:12)

"For the day of the Lord draws near on all the nations.
As you have done, it will be done to you.
Your dealings will return on your own head." (Ch.1:15)

THE MESSIANIC LINK:
The Messiah is *the deliverance from Zion* (Ch.1:21), the
True Judge.

THE BOOK:
This is the shortest book in the Old Testament, and one of
only 7 not mentioned in the New; although it is referred to
in Joel (Ch.2:32) and Jeremiah (Ch.49:14).
Obadiah (meaning *Servant of the Lord*) comes right to the
point here and preaches Judgment against the Edomites (the
descendants of Esau) for gloating over the persecution of
Judah.
The city of Jerusalem had been attacked by the Philistines
and Arabians. The city had been stormed and looted. Edom,

who was in a state of revolt, sided with the invading forces and shared in the spoils (Obad. 11). They gloated over Israel's misfortune (Obad. 12-13), and killed or imprisoned those who fled the destruction (Obad. 14).

Obadiah prophesies that they will be utterly destroyed in the 'Day of The Lord.'

NOTES & QUOTES:

The conflict between Edom and Israel is often used to visualize the battle that goes on in a Christian's life between the forces of evil (Edom) and the power of the Holy Spirit (Israel) in our lives.

The Apostle Paul , speaks about the fight between the flesh and the spirit that battles constantly within us (cf. Galatians 5:16–18 : Rom 7;24)

For the Christian, the fight against 'the flesh' or worldly desires goes on; it does not stop when you accept Jesus into your life.

The war against sin has already been won at the cross – but the battle against the flesh continues and will continue, until we finally meet with The Lord in Heaven.

******

Jonah:

WHEN:
Between 800 and 750 B.C.

WHO:

Traditionally attributed to Jonah son of Amittai; as indicated in the first verse.

PEOPLE & PLACES:
Jonah
Nineveh

SOUND-BITES:
And the Lord appointed a great fish to swallow Jonah, and Jonah was in the stomach of the fish three days and three nights. (Ch.1:17)

Then the Lord commanded the fish, and it vomited Jonah up onto the dry land. (Ch.2:10)

"Should I not have compassion on Nineveh, the great city in which there are more than 120,000 persons who do not know the difference between their right and left hand, as well as many animals?" (Ch.4:11)

THE MESSIANIC LINK:
Messiah typified in Jonah being three days and nights in the belly of the fish. (Ch.1:17. Matt.12:40)
Messianic prophecy in chapter 5 verse 2

THE BOOK:
The story begins with Jonah (meaning *Dove*) receiving a commission from God to go and preach repentance to the Ninevites, which he fears/loathes to do; so he runs away onto a ship going in the opposite direction!
After God whips up a storm and nearly sinks the ship, Jonah is thrown overboard and is swallowed by a large fish.
After three days and nights in the fish's belly he finally

repents, and the fish pukes him up on to the sea-shore possibly of Nineveh itself.

In chapter 3, Jonah's convincing preach causes the whole of Nineveh to believe his message and repent in sackcloth and ashes – much to Jonah's disgust, as he wanted God to punish them!

In the last chapter, Jonah tries to get God to change his mind by going into a sulk and asking to die; he was so unhappy. The book ends on an open-ended question – should God destroy the whole of Nineveh including 120,000 children as well as animals?

NOTES & QUOTES:

The main message from our friend Jonah is perhaps that you can run, but you cannot hide from God!

Jonah though he had good reason not to give The Lords message to the Ninevites – they were the sworn enemies of Israel, and Jonah seen no reason why they should not suffer the wrath of HIS God.

God however sees the bigger picture, and he is concerned about the many innocents that will suffer, should he destroy the city; and Jonah is the man he has chosen to deliver the message!

God can and does, call on all kinds of people to accomplish his will. This book tells the story of a reluctant prophet who arguably becomes one of the most effective preachers in the entire Bible – and he was not happy about it !

******

Micah:

WHEN:
Most likely between 725-710 B.C.

WHO:
Micah himself according to the first verse.

PEOPLE & PLACES:
Micah
Israel; Judah; Jerusalem; Bethlehem

SOUND-BITES:
Hear, O peoples, all of you;
Listen, O earth and all it contains,
And let the Lord God be a witness against you,
The Lord from His holy temple. (Ch.1:2)

"If a man walking after wind and falsehood
Had told lies and said,
'I will speak out to you concerning wine and liquor,'
He would be spokesman to this people. (Ch.2:11)

But as for me, I will watch expectantly for the Lord;
I will wait for the God of my salvation.
My God will hear me.
8. Do not rejoice over me, O my enemy.
Though I fall I will rise;
Though I dwell in darkness, the Lord is a light for me.
(Ch.7:7-8)

THE MESSIANIC LINK:
Messiah would be born in Bethlehem (Ch.5:2, Matt 2:1-2)

Messiah would be from everlasting (Ch.5:2, Rev:1-8)

THE BOOK:

Micah (meaning *'who is like unto The Lord,'* is another example of a common man whom God calls into the ministry of Prophet. He is a called to preach Judgement on the house of Judah as well as the imminent destruction of Samaria (Ch.1:2-15), owing to the corruption of priests and rulers who had lined their own pockets at the expense of the common people.

In fact he says that they are being ruled by a bunch of drunks and liars! (Ch.2:11).

The first three chapters indeed pronounce destruction, but the fourth chapter onwards points to happier times – upon repentance - of the restoration of Judah with peaceful days to come.

NOTES & QUOTES:

The Lord God hates injustice, corruption, false dealing as much as he hates the worship of false idols and the manipulation of his statutes and laws to suit our own ends !
The leaders of Micah's time were doing just that, they twisted the laws of the land to suit themselves, and no doubt called it piety !

Jesus condemned the same attitude in the Pharisees – the religious leaders of his time.

Are the times in which we live in, any different today?
The old adage that 'power corrupts, and absolute power corrupts absolutely' is as applicable now as it has been throughout the centuries from the beginning of time.

There is indeed - as the preacher says in the book of
Ecclesiastes – nothing new under the sun, and corruption is
as prevalent now as it ever was. It is also true that all it
needs for evil to succeed, is for good people to stand by and
do nothing while it is happening.

******

Nahum:

WHEN:
Between 663 and 612 B.C.

WHO:
Nahum the Elkoshite.

PEOPLE & PLACES:
Nahum
Nineveh; Judah; No-amon (Thebes)

SOUND-BITES:
"The Lord is slow to anger and great in power,
And the Lord will by no means leave the guilty
unpunished..." (Ch.1:3)

Your shepherds are sleeping, O king of Assyria;
Your nobles are lying down.
Your people are scattered on the mountains
And there is no one to regather them. (Ch.3:18)

THE MESSIANIC LINK:

The Messiah is reflected in 'Him who brings Good News.' (Ch.1:15. Rom.10:15)

THE BOOK:

Nahum is well named, as his name means 'consolation' which is in fact what the main theme of this book is about. Nahum comforts his people with the fact that God will punish the Ninevites for their evil-doing, against themselves and the surrounding nations.

This short book of only three chapters concentrates on the coming judgement of Nineveh by an angry God !! Including the destruction of the city itself, and the futility of trying to avoid or avert this judgement.

NOTES & QUOTES:

The Ninevites thought they had it all, and in fact behind their towering fortress walls they were unassailable. They were the most powerful and brutal Nation of their time, feared by everyone – or so they thought! They had been forgiven already under the preaching of Jonah some 150 years previously, but now they had reverted to their old ways and had decided they were out-with God's influence. However no-one is beyond the reach of God's Judgement, and He raised up the Babylonians under King Nebuchadnezzar to utterly destroy them.

Sometimes it is easy to feel that God is not listening, or that he is slow to take action. However His timing is perfect, and his Judgement against wickedness is guaranteed, as is His forgiveness upon true repentance. (2 Peter.3:8)

****

Habakkuk:

WHEN:
Written around 610 B.C.

WHO:
Attributed to Habakkuk (Ch.1:1; 3:1)

PEOPLE & PLACES:
Habakkuk
Chaldeans; Ninevites

SOUND-BITES:
"Look among the nations! Observe!
Be astonished! Wonder!
Because I am doing something in your days—
You would not believe if you were told." (Ch.1:5)

"For the earth will be filled
With the knowledge of the glory of the Lord,
As the waters cover the sea." (Ch.2:14)

But the righteous will live by his faith. (Ch.2:4)

Yet I will exult in the Lord,
I will rejoice in the God of my salvation. (Ch.3:18)

THE MESSIANIC LINK:
Typified in Habakkuk's life, (his intercession and prayer for his people).

Messianic link in Chapter 2 v 4 '... But the righteous will
live by his faith.'

THE BOOK:

Habakkuk (meaning *embraces* or *clings to*) concentrates on
the three main points, as God has revealed them.
The coming destruction by the Babylonians; of the
rebellious people of Judah. (1:5-11)
Judgement on the Surrounding nations. (1:4-18)
Restoration of the remnant. (3:12,13)
He begins in chapter 1 by asking God through petition and
prayer, why it is that the wicked prosper and the righteous
suffer; and God answers him, saying that he is about to
raise up the Chaldeans to punish the wicked.
In chapter 2, the theme of God's righteous Judgement
against the wickedness of the nations is continued.
The book ends with Habakkuk acknowledging that God is
just and righteous, and his decisions cannot be disputed.
(Ch.3:17-19)

NOTES & QUOTES:

What makes Habakkuk unusual is that most prophesies
God address's the people through the Prophets, but here
Habakkuk addresses God directly – no other prophet starts
this way.
Habakkuk even dares to question the plans of The Lord to
use the Babylonians to administer judgement on Judah,
admitting a little concern or confusion over God's plans.
(1:13)

We all know about **intercessory** prayer - Habakkuk gives us an example of **interrogatory** prayer – where we ask questions of God …..Why do the wicked prosper?

Most of us, if we are honest, sort of skirt around any questions we have regarding The Lords desires or purposes. Often we really do not feel that 'spiritual justice' has been done, and yet we do not dare to ask God about it.

Habakkuk however had no such concerns – why? Because he knew more than anyone that The Lord reads the heart, more than he listens to your voice sometimes.

Important point however – we ask questions of God – we do NOT question him!

******

Zephaniah:

WHEN:
Most likely around 725 B.C.

WHO:
Zephaniah himself. (Ch.1:1)

PEOPLE & PLACES:
Zephaniah
Jerusalem; Canaan; Philistines; Moab; Israel.

SOUND-BITES:
Be silent before the Lord God!
For the day of the Lord is near,
For the Lord has prepared a sacrifice,

He has consecrated His guests. (Ch.1:7)

"At that time I will bring you in,
Even at the time when I gather you together;
Indeed, I will give you renown and praise
Among all the peoples of the earth,
When I restore your fortunes before your eyes,"
Says the Lord. (Ch.3:20)

THE MESSIANIC LINK:
The Messiah is 'The Restorer' in Chapter 3:14-20)

THE BOOK:
The Prophet Zephaniah (name meaning 'conceals'); in this short book of only 3 chapters, has a message of Judgement to deliver to the Nations surrounding Judah, and ultimately Judah itself.

Judgement on the nations East and West
Zeph 2:4-7 Philistia.
Zeph 2:8-11 Moab & Amon.
Judgement on nations South and North
Zeph 2:12 Ethiopia. "You also Ethiopians will be slain by the sword"
Zeph 2:13-15 Assyria.
Judgement on Jerusalem . Zeph 3:1-4
However he finishes on a positive note, pronouncing God's blessing in the last chapter of the book. (Ch.3:14-17)

NOTES & QUOTES:
The book of Zephaniah follows the pattern of the Four R's Rebellion, Retribution, Repentance, Restoration. So often found in the teachings of the prophets of Israel.

1.   **Rebellion:** The people rebel against the teachings of the Lord or his servants the Prophets.

2.   **Retribution:** The Lord exacts retribution or judgement against them.

3.   **Repentance:** The people see the error of their ways – leading to repentance, or a 'turning away' from evil.

4.   **Restoration:** When the people finally see the error of their ways and repent, then The Lord is able (and willing) to restore fully.

This emphasizes the fact that God does not punish because he takes some perverse delight in it! But rather rebellion will lead to Him exacting retribution in order to encourage repentance; so that he is then able to forgive and restore the Individual or Nation.

******

Haggai:

WHEN:
Around 520 B.C.

WHO:
Traditionally attributed to Haggai himself.

PEOPLE & PLACES:
Haggai; Zerubbabel; Joshua son of Jehozadak; Darius
Judah

SOUND-BITES:

Then the word of the Lord came by Haggai the prophet, saying, "Is it time for you yourselves to dwell in your paneled houses while this house lies desolate?" (Ch.1:3-4) 'The latter glory of this house will be greater than the former,' says the Lord of hosts, 'and in this place I will give peace,' declares the Lord of hosts." (Ch.2:9)

THE MESSIANIC LINK:
Messiah is the 'Signet Ring' in Ch.2:23 in the line of Zerubbabel.

THE BOOK:

Haggai (meaning *festive*) is another short book of only 2 chapters this time, but one that is full of challenge for the people who had returned to Jerusalem, and made nice houses for themselves and yet ignored the 'House of The Lord.' He asked them if it was any wonder that they did not prosper as they should, seeing that they had ignored God's house (Ch.1:6-9).

However with repentance and application to the House of The Lord, then God would prosper them and restore their fortunes. He would prosper them materially and with vengeance against their enemies, ultimately finishing with God's blessing on their leader Zerubbabel whom He would make his 'signet ring.'

NOTES & QUOTES:
The book of Haggai gives us a clear example of just how easy it is to get caught up in our own everyday lives, to the detriment of our relationship with The Lord. The Jews had

become pre-occupied with their own needs, upon return to a devastated Jerusalem; forgetting that it was The Lord who had made the return possible in the first place.

Here we have an instance though of God's mercy, when he made it plain through Haggai, just what the problem was, and how they could rectify it by simply attending to The Lord who is the one who will restore their fortunes 'before their eyes.' (Ch.2:20)

******

Zechariah:

WHEN:
Around the same time as Haggai – 520 B.C.

WHO:
Attributed to Zechariah in Ch.1:1

PEOPLE & PLACES:
Zechariah; Zerubbabel; Jerusalem
Babylon; Judah

SOUND-BITES:
Therefore say to them, 'Thus says the Lord of hosts, "Return to Me," declares the Lord of hosts, "that I may return to you," says the Lord of hosts. (Ch.1:3)

And just as He called and they would not listen, so they called and I would not listen," says the Lord of hosts; (Ch.7:13)

"In that day a fountain will be opened for the house of David and for the inhabitants of Jerusalem, for sin and for impurity." (Ch.13:1)

"...They will call on My name,
And I will answer them;
I will say, 'They are My people,'
And they will say, 'The Lord is my God." (Ch.13:9)

THE MESSIANIC LINK:
He is The Righteous Branch --- 3:8; 6:12-13
Messiah would be Priest and King (Zech 6:12-13)
He will ride into Jerusalem on a donkey (Zech 9:9)
The cornerstone, tent peg, & bow of battle --- 10:4
He will be God (Zech 11:12-13, John 12:45)
Messiah would be pierced (Zech 12:10, John 19:34-37)
The coming Judge & righteous King --- chapter 14

THE BOOK:
No other prophet with the exception of Isaiah spoke more about the Messiah than Zechariah. The book is predominantly Apocalyptic and Eschatological and through his prophesies he manages to put a real awareness and eagerness into the hearts of the people with his messages of Messianic hope.
Zechariah follows in the same vein as Haggai, in that the book is dedicated throughout to bringing the people to repentance and an awareness of the importance of The Lord in their ultimate restoration.

Symbolism and allegory place a large part in Zechariah's messages such as Golden lampstands (Ch.4), flying scrolls (Ch.5) and the Four Chariots in chapter 6.

The book ends with God himself battling with their enemies, and being exalted as 'King over all the Earth' in chapter 14.

NOTES & QUOTES:

I believe the main thrust of Zechariah's message-the coming of the Lord-is what should drive us today, even more so than it drove the Israelites in Zechariah's time. The message of the new testament is crammed full of passages relating to the return of Christ in Power and Glory. The 'Suffering servant' has been and gone, we now await his return as the coming Judge and Righteous King (ch:14).

Eschatology – the study of the end times – is a subject that is by and large ignored today and yet the early church thought of little else. As a result the church grew at an exponential rate. This anticipation made a fertile bed for Paul and the early Apostles to sow the seeds of the Gospel message into.

******

Malachi:

WHEN:

Between 440 and 400 B.C. most likely.

WHO:
Malachi himself is accredited in the first verse, though some feel Ezra is the writer.

PEOPLE & PLACES:
Malachi
Judah; Priesthood

SOUND-BITES:
"'A son honors his father, and a servant his master. Then if I am a father, where is My honor? And if I am a master, where is My respect?' says the Lord of hosts to you, O priests who despise My name. But you say, 'How have we despised Your name?' (Ch.1:6)

You have wearied the Lord with your words. Yet you say, "How have we wearied Him?" In that you say, "Everyone who does evil is good in the sight of the Lord, and He delights in them," or, "Where is the God of justice?" (Ch.2:17)

"Will a man rob God? Yet you are robbing Me! But you say, 'How have we robbed You?' In tithes and offerings." (Ch.3:8)

THE MESSIANIC LINK:
He is The Lord in the Temple. (Ch.3:2) and the 'messenger of the covenant in Ch.3:3.

THE BOOK:
Malachi (meaning '*messenger*'), Enters the scene as the people of Judah had reached a spiritual all-time low. The Temple had been re-built as well as the walls of Jerusalem,

but apathy and corruption had seeped into every aspect of life – even the priesthood. God sent Malachi to warn of the consequences if the situation was not put right.

Throughout the book Malachi warns them of their coming Judgement for continuing to disobey and dishonor God; leading to the coming of the messenger in Chapter 3, who will 'clear the way.'

The fourth and final chapter ends on a high note, promising them victory over their enemies.

NOTES & QUOTES:

The people on their return to the 'Promised land' were set a great challenge, to re-build a ruined country.

After granted a fair amount of prodding they set about it and got on with the task of re-building the Temple and the city walls.

But look what happens when the task is completed.

Boredom – We've done our job, now what?

Apathy – let's just do our religious duty then get on with real life!

Rebelliousness - Look at our neighbors the Canaanites, they're partying and having a great time of it!!

We need purpose in our lives – we need the reality of God to rule in our lives and we need more than anything a God Given Goal a vision, a revelation, a dream that the Lord would plant in our hearts, we need to fulfill the destiny that The Lord has planned for us otherwise, like the people of Israel we will wander off into the sunset and slide into apathy and rebellion.

******

NEW TESTAMENT
(Covenant)

INTRO:

The New Testament or 'Covenant' refers to a new relationship between God and man, now united through the last blood sacrifice, Jesus - Gods own Son. Often referred to as the Lamb of God, Jesus is 'the acceptable sacrifice' who offers salvation to all that believe on Him. Through the 27 books of the New Testament, the 'Old' is unveiled to reveal a perfect salvation based on Grace & Faith in Christ, rather than an imperfect deliverance based on the Law of the Old Testament.

We are now in 'The Age of Grace,' the world of the New Testament; an age that offers salvation to Jew and gentile alike, not through the law or sacrifice but through belief and faith in Jesus Christ only.

Matthew:

WHEN:

Just before or around A.D. 70

WHO:

Traditionally ascribed to Matthew.

PEOPLE & PLACES:

Jesus; Herod; John the Baptist; The Twelve Disciples; Pilate; Sadducee's; Pharisee's

Bethlehem; Jerusalem; Galilee; Judea.

SOUND-BITES:

..and behold, a voice out of the heavens said, "This is My beloved Son, in whom I am well-pleased." (Ch.3:17)

But He answered and said, "It is written, 'Man shall not live on bread alone, but on every word that proceeds out of the mouth of God.'" (Ch.4:4)

For what will it profit a man if he gains the whole world and forfeits his soul? Or what will a man give in exchange for his soul? (Ch.16:26)

The angel said to the women, "Do not be afraid; for I know that you are looking for Jesus who has been crucified. **6.** He is not here, for He has risen, just as He said. Come, see the place where He was lying. (Ch.28:5-6)

THE MESSIANIC LINK:
The Messiah is the Son of David (Matt 1:1)
He would born of God (Ch.1:18, Isaiah.7:14)
The King of the Jews (Matthew 2:2)
He would return from Egypt. (Matt.2:15. Hosea.11:1)
Messiah is the *Narrow Gate* (Ch.7:13)
Messiah is the bridegroom in chapter 9

THE BOOK:
The main purpose of Matthew is to convince the Jewish people that Jesus is indeed the King and Messiah that was promised throughout the Old Testament writings. He goes to great lengths to point out the genealogy of Jesus, thereby qualifying his 'claim to the title' of Messiah (savior).

The first 17 verses of the first chapter lays out his birth line, so as to leave no doubt as to his credentials, as put forward by the writers of old.

Thereafter Matthew concentrates on the life and works of Jesus, in particular equating his miracles with the Old Testament prophecies relating to the life and death of the coming Messiah; this he uses as evidence of Jesus as Messiah.

Chapter 10 sees the naming and instruction of the Twelve Disciples for service. Whilst chapters 14-20 covers the ministry of Jesus throughout the land of Galilee and Judea.

The final chapters 27 and 28 culminate in the Crucifixion, Death and Resurrection of Jesus.

NOTES & QUOTES:

As an introduction to New Testament Christianity, the book of Matthew is excellent, as it is laid out in a very straight-forward logical way that is easy to follow.

As a guide to where Jesus was mentioned in the Old Testament; it is again an excellent book for revealing how Jesus was in fact the fulfillment of the Old Testament prophecies relating to his birth, death and ministry while he walked amongst us.

Matthew had a hard time convincing the Jewish leadership amongst the Pharisee's and Sadducees, of Jesus authority, as they had already constructed their own image of what he would be like when he appeared – and Jesus did not fit the bill, even though the evidence was right before their eyes!

It is easy to get ourselves locked into pre-conceptions of the way things should be – leaving us open to rejecting the truth when it is not 'wearing the coat' we have made for it.

The evidence pointing to Jesus as the promised Messiah is overwhelming, and in accordance with scriptural promises; and yet some people just want more evidence – go figure!

******

Mark:

WHEN:
Most likely between A.D. 55-60

WHO:
Traditionally ascribed to Mark

PEOPLE & PLACES:
Jesus; The Twelve Disciples; John the Baptist; Bartimaeus;
Herod; Pilate
Nazareth; Gethsemane

SOUND-BITES:
and a voice came out of the heavens: "You are My beloved
Son, in You I am well-pleased." (Ch.1:11)

Jesus said to them, "A prophet is not without honor except
in his hometown and among his own relatives and in his
own household." (Ch.6:4)

Then Judas Iscariot, who was one of the twelve, went off to
the chief priests in order to betray Him to them. (Ch.14:10)

And He said to them, "Go into all the world and preach the
gospel to all creation. **16.** He who has believed and has
been baptized shall be saved; but he who has disbelieved
shall be condemned. (Ch.16:15-16)

THE MESSIANIC LINK:
He is 'The Holy One of God' in Mark 1:24

The 'Suffering Servant' of Mark 10:45
The 'Son of God' in Mark 15:39

THE BOOK:

Since the book of Mark is not aimed primarily at the Jews, he does not go into the same detail regarding Jesus connection with the Old Testament prophecies (although this aspect is covered numerous times); but rather he emphasizes the works and wonders surrounding Jesus ministry.

Chapter one introduces us to John the Baptist, and the baptism of Jesus himself, then goes straight to the wilderness experience; after which Jesus returns and appoints fishermen Simon and Andrew as his first followers.

The first demon is cast out in chapter 1, followed by miraculous healings of many kinds in the subsequent chapters. Chapter 4 sees the parables of the sower and the Mustard seed, as well as Jesus taking control over the seas. In chapter 6 he feeds the five thousand and in chapter 8 the four thousand.

Mark continues by illustrating the miraculous nature of Christ's ministry, which culminates in his betrayal by Judas (Ch.14:45), crucifixion and resurrection (Chaps.15,16). The book finishes on the ascension of Christ to the right hand of God, and the Apostles preaching the Word with signs and wonders following.

NOTES & QUOTES:

The book of Mark promotes the 'Suffering Servant' aspect of Jesus ministry, and he exhorts us to follow His example in that regard (Ch.10:45). This is perhaps an aspect of Jesus ministry that most of us are not too keen on – if truth be told! The fact is however that whilst I am not into self-immolation in any way – nor is it called for – there is an argument for suffering alongside those we are trying to help, before we can truly empathise with their situation.

Jesus was not afraid to get his hands dirty, when it came to His ministry; nor was he afraid of what people said – even the religious leaders of the time. He led by example, and exhorts us to do the same.

If we desire to be 'great' in God's kingdom, then we must be willing to serve in this one (Ch.10:44).

******

Luke:

WHEN:
Between A.D. 59 and 65

WHO:
Traditionally ascribed to Luke

PEOPLE & PLACES:
Jesus; Luke; John the Baptist; Mary; Martha; Lazarus;
Bartimaeus; Judas; Pilot; Herod
Nazareth; Gethsemane;

SOUND-BITES:

For today in the city of David there has been born for you a Savior, who is Christ the Lord. (Ch.2:11)

And Jesus answered him, "It is written, 'Man shall not live on bread alone.'" (Ch.4:4)

Why do you look at the speck that is in your brother's eye, but do not notice the log that is in your own eye? (Ch.6:41)

…."Blessed is the King who comes in the name of the Lord; Peace in heaven and glory in the highest!" (Ch.19:38)

And as the women were terrified and bowed their faces to the ground, the men said to them, "Why do you seek the living One among the dead? **6.** He is not here, but He has risen. Remember how He spoke to you while He was still in Galilee (Ch.24:5-6).

THE MESSIANIC LINK:
He is the Horn of Salvation (Luke 1:69)
The Consolation of Israel: (Luke 2:25)

THE BOOK:
As the first four verses of Luke attests, this book aims to give a detailed account of the person and ministry of Jesus, laid out in an orderly fashion for the reader to easily understand. Aimed primarily at the Gentiles, he records particularly the parables and Jesus' interest in the poor and oppressed of all nations.

This includes the Centurion's servant, and a widow's son (Ch.7:1-15); one about to die and the other already dead! Both of whom Jesus had compassion upon, and healed completely.

The first four chapters of Luke can be described as the preparation for His ministry, and the chapters 4 – 19 the record of this miraculous ministry in Galilee, Judea and Perea

Chapters 19 – 24 start from the Triumphal Entry into Jerusalem, and the events leading up to His crucifixion, resurrection and ministry to the Apostles; before his ascension up to Heaven.

NOTES & QUOTES:

Luke is described by some as the most beautiful book in the New Testament, and with good reason. It is well written out in orderly fashion, by a man who was most probably a physician of Gentile birth; and someone who obviously had a real concern for the 'common people.'

The main focus of this book is that of Jesus the healer and comforter, as well as a good teller of parables; through which He instructs them on many aspects of life both physical and spiritual.

'Gospel' means 'Good News,' and Luke certainly gives us that, with a true and honest account of Jesus life in a beautifully presented order.

******

John:

WHEN:
Around A.D. 85

Who:

The Apostle John

People & Places:

Jesus; John; John the Baptist; Mary; Lazarus; Judas; Pilate; Galilee; Bethesda;

Sound-Bites:

In the beginning was the Word, and the Word was with God, and the Word was God. (Ch.1:1)

The next day he *saw Jesus coming to him and *said, "Behold, the Lamb of God who takes away the sin of the world! (Ch.1:29)

"For God so loved the world, that He gave His only begotten Son, that whoever believes in Him shall not perish, but have eternal life. (Ch.3:16)

The thief comes only to steal and kill and destroy; I came that they may have life, and have it abundantly. (Ch.10:10)

Jesus *said to him, "I am the way, and the truth, and the life; no one comes to the Father but through Me. (Ch.14:6)

But these have been written so that you may believe that Jesus is the Christ, the Son of God; and that believing you may have life in His name. (Ch.20:31)

The Messianic Link:

He is the Only Begotten Son: (John 1:14,18) And the Lamb of God (John 1:29,36)
In John 6:35 He is the Bread of Life
He is The Light of the World (John 8:1)

The I AM! Of John 8:58
The Door of the Sheep: (John 10:7,9)
The Good Shepherd (John 10:11)
The Way, the Truth, and the Life (John 14:6)
The True Vine (John 15:1)

THE BOOK:

John begins this book, with emphasis on the Deity of Jesus; which is indeed is a theme which is maintained throughout. Jesus it the ''True Light' which has come into the world, and as such John is testifying that He is the 'Only Begotten' of The Father; emphasizing both his humanity and his Deity.

In chapter 5 John explains Jesus' equality with God, and how this started the real conflict with the religious leaders at the time. Jesus affirms his Deity in chapter 9:35-41 and chapter 10:25-30; and continues in this vein through-out the rest of the book.

After performing His first miracle – turning water into wine in chapter 2 – Jesus continues to perform many more; including healing a noble man's son (Ch.4:46-54), healing the cripple at Bethsaida (Ch.5:1-9), and feeding the 5,000 (Ch.6:1-14).

From chapter 13 onwards, John writes about Jesus' preparing the disciple's for his death and ultimate resurrection.

John finishes by declaring that there were many other things which Jesus did, but that he could not record owing to the sheer volume involved.

NOTES & QUOTES:

I think it's fair to say that most Christians have a 'special' book within the 66 books that make up the Bible; and indeed I am no exception!

John was the book that spoke loudly to me, on the night that I really sought The Lord for salvation. The words are emotive and 'real' in a way that makes this book stand out to people and speaks to the heart, perhaps more than the head – in my opinion!

As well as promoting the Deity of Jesus, this book really promotes relationship through Him with God The Father. 'The Good Shepherd' and 'Light of the world' promotes Jesus as someone who cares for, and can identify with, the trials that we go through as individuals.

John himself emphasizes his reasons for writing this book when he says.. "But these have been written so that you may believe that Jesus is the Christ, the Son of God; and that believing you may have life in His name. (Ch.20:31)

It certainly works for me!

******

Acts:

WHEN:
Likely between A.D. 60-65

WHO:
Traditionally ascribed to Luke

PEOPLE & PLACES:

Jesus; Saul (Paul); Peter; Silas; John; Cornelius; Barnabas; Simeon; Herod; Agrippa; Festus
Jerusalem; Judea; Samaria; Athens; Corinth; Ephesus; Macedonia; Caesarea;

SOUND-BITES:

"But you will receive power when the Holy Spirit has come upon you; and you shall be My witnesses both in Jerusalem, and in all Judea and Samaria, and even to the remotest part of the earth." (Ch.1:8)

"And there is salvation in no one else; for there is no other name under heaven that has been given among men by which we must be saved." (Ch.4:12)

They said, "Believe in the Lord Jesus, and you will be saved, you and your household." (Ch.16:31)

And Paul said, "I would wish to God, that whether in a short or long time, not only you, but also all who hear me this day, might become such as I am, except for these chains." (Ch.26:29)

And he fell to the ground and heard a voice saying to him, "Saul, Saul, why are you persecuting Me?" **5**. And he said, "Who are You, Lord?" And He said, "I am Jesus whom you are persecuting. (Ch.9:4-5)

THE MESSIANIC LINK:

He is the Prince of Life in Acts 3:15
He is the Righteous One in Acts 7:52
The Judge of the living and the dead (Acts 10:42)

THE BOOK:

The book of Acts gives us a history of the work of the early church and the Holy Spirit, within the theatre of the known world. From the empowering by the Holy Spirit in chapter 2, the early church made a great impact on all it encountered; the Apostles Peter and John playing a major role in this early work. The great persecutor of the Christians, Saul; had a tremendous conversion on the road to Damascus (Ch.9) after which he was known as Paul. Chapters 13 – 29 continues with the first of three missionary journeys as Paul and the Apostles/Church members, spread the word in accordance with Acts 1:8; meeting the opposition of Jew and Gentile with stoicism and faith in God.

NOTES & THOUGHTS:

The book of Acts is one of the most exciting and challenging of the new Testament, filled as it is with the works of the early church, empowered by the Holy Spirit. The 'tongues of fire' and rushing wind on the day of Pentecost (Ch.2), as well as 'speaking in other tongues;' an outward sign and witness to the onlookers that The Lord was with them. A witness that resulted in 3,000 conversions at a single meeting!

Could it be that a large part of the problem with empty pews today, is that there is nothing to see or hear in some churches that warrants a second look?

******

Romans:

WHEN:
Around A.D.55-58

WHO:
The Apostle Paul (Ch.1:1)

PEOPLE & PLACES:
Christ; Paul (Tertius)
Israel; Rome

SOUND-BITES:
For I am not ashamed of the gospel, for it is the power of God for salvation to everyone who believes, to the Jew first and also to the Greek. (Ch.1:16)

For all have sinned and fall short of the glory of God. (Ch.3:23)

And we know that God causes all things to work together for good to those who love God, to those who are called according to His purpose. (Ch.8:28)

…that if you confess with your mouth Jesus as Lord, and believe in your heart that God raised Him from the dead, you will be saved. (Ch.10:9)

THE MESSIANIC LINK:
He is the Stumbling Stone (Romans 9:33)
The Deliverer from Zion (Romans 11:26)
The Lord of the dead and the living (Romans 14:9)

The Root of Jesse who rules over the Gentiles (Romans 15:12)

THE BOOK:

Romans is a book of Doctrine, Christian living and Justification by Faith alone (Chaps.3,4). Paul begins by warning of the consequences of unbelief in chapter 1; warning that all men are guilty under the Law (Ch.3:23), and so needing redemption through faith in Christ. From chapter 4 onwards he warns that the Old Testament law has failed, in that it was only ever intended to lead people to the perfect law, which is through faith in Christ (Ch.10:17). Chapter 12 onward instructs on Christian living, service and conscience (Ch.14), with regard to eating habits and condemning others for what they do, or do not eat.

NOTES & QUOTES:

There is perhaps no other book in the New Testament, with the exception of the four Gospels, that have had such an impact on Church history; and in particular the period of the reformation.

Augustine's conversion is largely due to Romans, as is the 'Justification by Faith alone' movement of Martin Luther, that started the great Reformation and the Protestant movement.

Many issues are covered from Diet and Conscience Ch.14) to homosexuality (Ch.1:24-28); very much a 'hot topic' in our own day.

In Romans 7:14-25, Paul exorcises his mighty brain and writes down what is arguably the most confusing chapter ever written through-out the New Testament – and a great topic for discussion in any house group!

******

1 Corinthians:

WHEN:
Around A.D.55

WHO:
Paul himself (Ch.1:1)

PEOPLE & PLACES:
Christ; Paul; Apollos
Corinth; Ephesus;

SOUND-BITES:
For the word of the cross is foolishness to those who are perishing, but to us who are being saved it is the power of God. (Ch.1:18)

Or do you not know that your body is a temple of the Holy Spirit who is in you, whom you have from God, and that you are not your own? **20.** For you have been bought with a price: therefore glorify God in your body. (Ch.6:19,20)

In a moment, in the twinkling of an eye, at the last trumpet; for the trumpet will sound, and the dead will be raised imperishable, and we will be changed. (Ch.15:52)

THE MESSIANIC LINK:

He is the First-fruits of 1 Corinthians 15:23; and the Last Adam 15:47.

The Book:

Paul writes to the Church at Corinth, primarily to address a number of issues and divisions amongst the people; beginning with disunity in chapter 1 brought on by 'cliques' forming over who had been baptized by whom. They had also succumbed to the temptations of Corinth, in a way that was not acceptable, and so Paul had to exhort and rebuke in alternate measure in order to get them to understand the error of their ways. In chapter 10 he reminds them of Israel's failings, and the Judgement of God upon them.

Even their use of the Spiritual gifts was not being exercised properly (Ch.12), leading to some thinking they were superior to others; he points out that without love, then it is all of no account (Ch.13).

Notes & Quotes:

The issues that faced the Corinthian church, especially with regard to immorality, in my opinion, are mirrored in the age in which we live. In fact with the advent of the Internet and free access to all sorts of pornographic material, as well as the temptations of the world that are put before us on TV screens that are more and more explicit; I would say that Christian values are truly 'under the Cosh' so to speak.

The Church has to get its act together and promote a Gospel that is relevant and exciting, as well as morally acceptable, if it is to encourage and influence people –

especially the youth - in today's world. The difficulties that people have with temptations of all kinds, was something that Paul understood perfectly, and something that we have to tackle earnestly in today's Church, if we are to see it prosper and influence our communities in a positive way.

******

2 Corinthians:

WHEN:
Around A.D.55

WHO:
Paul himself

PEOPLE & PLACES:
Christ; Paul; Timothy
Corinth; Jerusalem

SOUND-BITES:
But we all, with unveiled face, beholding as in a mirror the glory of the Lord, are being transformed into the same image from glory to glory, just as from the Lord, the Spirit. (Ch.3:18)

Therefore if anyone is in Christ, he is a new creature; the old things passed away; behold, new things have come. (Ch.5:17)

For it is not he who commends himself that is approved, but he whom the Lord commends. (Ch.10:18)

The Messianic Link:
As in 1 Corinthians: He is the First-fruits of 1 Corinthians 15:23; and the Last Adam 15:47.

THE BOOK:

Paul begins this letter by re-iterating his call to the Apostleship, and emphasizing the trials and tribulations he has been through for the Gospels sake. He explains the reasons behind his travel plans, while at the same time defending his integrity against those within the Church that would seek to undermine him.

Chapter 3 through to 7 sees Paul preaching and ministering the New Covenant of 'the righteousness of Christ' against the old 'ministry of condemnation' (Ch.3:9).

In Chapters 6 and 7 , Paul goes on to defend his ministry, emphasizing the severe persecution he has been put through for the Gospels sake; while at the same time assuring the Corinthians of his sincere love for them.

In chapters 8-9 he discusses the aspect of giving to the ministry, emphasizing the need to give with a cheerful heart (Ch.9:7)

He finishes his letter by further defending his position of authority over them, and pleading with them to examine themselves; lest they themselves should fail the test. (13:5)

NOTES & QUOTES:

In this second letter to the Corinthian church, Paul is again having to deal with internal issues, and problems with people within the church trying to undermine his own ministry; even to the point of doubting his authority and calling.

The fact that he feels it necessary to prove himself (Ch.12), irritates him to the point that he calls himself a 'fool' for doing so.

It would be great to think that the Church of the past, was all 'sweetness and love;' the fact is however that even from its conception there has been internal trouble. The reason for this? Simple; although perfected in spirit, we are not perfect at heart and still battle against the 'old man' inside. Check out Romans 7:14-25, if you are in any doubt!

The fact is though, that we are the Church that God in his wisdom has decided to use for His Glory – and he does not make mistakes!

******

Galatians:

WHEN:
Around A.D. 50

WHO:
The Apostle Paul (Ch.1:1)

PEOPLE & PLACES:
Christ; Paul; Peter (Cephas)
Galatia; Jerusalem

SOUND-BITES:

I am amazed that you are so quickly deserting Him who called you by the grace of Christ, for a different gospel; 7. which is really not another; only there are some who are disturbing you and want to distort the gospel of Christ. (Ch.1:6-7)

"Nevertheless knowing that a man is not justified by the works of the Law but through faith in Christ Jesus..." (Ch.2:16)

But the fruit of the Spirit is love, joy, peace, patience, kindness, goodness, faithfulness, **23.** gentleness, self-control; against such things there is no law. (Ch.5:22-23)

Do not be deceived, God is not mocked; for whatever a man sows, this he will also reap. (Ch.6:7)

THE MESSIANIC LINK:
He is the One Who Rescues us (Ch.1:3-4)

THE BOOK:
In this letter to the Galatian church, Paul is up against the 'Judaizers' that is to say; Jews who have converted to Christianity but still place value in the old laws of The Torah – particularly circumcision.

In the first chapter he expresses amazement that they have so easily reverted back to the 'old ways;' a system of salvation through the keeping of the law.

From verse 11 of the first chapter he goes on to defend his Ministry and his calling, taught to him by direct revelation from Jesus Christ (Ch.1:12). He condemns even Peter and Barnabas for being a hypocrite and siding with the Jewish faction (Ch.2:11-14), and continues in the following chapters to emphasize with great earnestness the salvation they have received.

It is a salvation based on grace and faith (Ch.3 onwards), and has no connection to the works of the law to which they were once subject.

He finishes his letter by encouraging them to 'bear one another's burdens' and in this way alone 'fulfill the law of Christ.' (Ch.6)

NOTES & QUOTES:

The Galatian church had fallen into the old trap of trying hard to earn their salvation – which is basically what following the old law was all about.

Even today however, individuals can be sucked into the whole idea that they have to earn what The Lord has freely given them. It is in our nature to expect to 'pay' for something, and so easy for us to fall into the trap that God expects payment in some manner or other.

It was easy for the Jewish contingent of the Galatian church to insist that they must follow certain laws – such as circumcision for men – because the people had not truly grasped the idea of salvation through faith in Christ alone. We must always be on our guard against individuals who may insist on us following certain diets, or dress code, or even perform certain duties; in order to appropriate what God **has already given us** through faith in Christ. (Ch.3:11)

******

Ephesians:

WHEN:
Around A.D. 60

WHO:
Traditionally ascribed to Paul

PEOPLE & PLACES:
Christ; Paul; Tychicus

SOUND-BITES:
—having also believed, you were sealed in Him with the Holy Spirit of promise. (Ch.1:13)

For by grace you have been saved through faith; and that not of yourselves, it is the gift of God. (Ch.2:8)

Now to Him who is able to do far more abundantly beyond all that we ask or think, according to the power that works within us. (Ch.3:20)

Therefore be careful how you walk, not as unwise men but as wise. (Ch.5:15)

THE MESSIANIC LINK:
He is the Head over All Things (Ephesians 1:22) and the Cornerstone in Ephesians 2:20

THE BOOK:
Paul starts of this letter by greeting the church at Ephesus, who unlike the church at Corinth, are predominantly Gentiles and get along very well, but have need of further teaching in order to mature as Christians in the Faith.

Chapters 1 and 2 encourage them to understand the depth of their conversion, that they have been 'made alive' (Ch.2:5) through Grace alone.

In the following chapters he encourages the Ephesian church to work as a family, and look to their brothers and sisters needs before their own, and to walk in a manner worthy of their calling (Ch.4:1).

He finishes his letter in chapter 6 with a dire warning about the wiles of the enemy, and the need to always look to God for protection and deliverance; to 'put on the full armor of God' (Ch.6:10-18) in order to defeat him and stand 'in the evil day' of persecution.

NOTES & QUOTES:

The book of Ephesians is an excellent read for anyone who is unsure of their standing in Christ. The fact that they are 'sealed in Him' (Ch.1:13) should be enough in itself to convince the reader that on repentance and confession of Faith in Christ, they are indeed heaven-bound.

This letter is however probably better known for the 'Armor of God' passages in chapter 6; and not without good reason.

Often we are persuaded to believe that our troubles come from the things that we can see with our 5 senses. Paul makes it clear however that this is not the case, there are spiritual forces at work amongst us, and what we find with our own senses are a mere reflection of what is really going on in the spiritual dimension.

To take control of our physical circumstances – we must first of all prepare ourselves in the spiritual realm with 'prayer and petition' in the Spirit.

******

Philippians:

WHEN:
About A.D 61

WHO:
The Apostle Paul (Ch.1:1)

PEOPLE & PLACES:
Christ; Paul; Timothy; Epaphroditus
Philippi

SOUND-BITES:
For to me, to live is Christ and to die is gain. (Ch.1:21)

..so that at the name of Jesus every knee will bow, of those who are in heaven and on earth and under the earth, **11.** and that every tongue will confess that Jesus Christ is Lord, to the glory of God the Father. (Ch.2:10-11)

Rejoice in the Lord always; again I will say, rejoice! (Ch.4:4)

And my God will supply all your needs according to His riches in glory in Christ Jesus. (Ch.4:19)

THE MESSIANIC LINK:

He is the *Name above every name* (Ch.2:9)

THE BOOK:

Written during Paul's imprisonment in Rome, this is
sometimes known as the prison letter. Rather than
bemoaning his situation however, this letter concentrates on
the joy of knowing the Lord.

Throughout this epistle Paul encourages the Philippians to
rejoice in the Lord, whatever circumstances they are in
because in this way they can become an effective witness
for Christ (Ch.1:18).

Chapter 3 onward encourages them to 'press on towards the
goal' and to think of excellence, being anxious for nothing.
The letter finishes with Paul thanking them for their gifts
and commending the to God in prayer.

NOTES & QUOTES:

The letter to the Philippians is a valuable reminder that God
is in our situation, no matter where we are or how bad it
seems. Paul had learned to praise God no matter what his
circumstances, and in this letter encourages us to do the
same; for who knows just what impact our witness may
have?

******

Colossians:

WHEN:

Likely written between A.D. 58-60

Who:

The Apostle Paul

People & Places:

Christ; Paul; Timothy; Aristarchus;

Sound-Bites:

He is the image of the invisible God, the firstborn of all creation. (Ch.1:15)

Therefore as you have received Christ Jesus the Lord, so walk in Him. (Ch.2:6)

Therefore if you have been raised up with Christ, keep seeking the things above, where Christ is, seated at the right hand of God. (Ch.3:1)

Conduct yourselves with wisdom toward outsiders, making the most of the opportunity. (Ch.4:5)

The Messianic Link:

He is the Image of the Invisible God (Colossians 1:15)
The Head of the body, the Beginning, and the Firstborn from the dead (Colossians 1:18)
The Hope of Glory (Col 1:27)

The Book:

Paul begins his letter to the Colossian church, with greetings and thanks giving's, however he is soon onto the main purpose; which is to counter heresy that had been making some headway amongst the members.
In chapter 2 he exhorts them not to be led astray with deceptive argument or indeed to pay attention to 'human

philosophy' but instead to consider the absolute sufficiency of Christ.

Chapter 3 & 4 encourages the believers to deal fairly with one another, and to deal wisely with outsiders (Ch.4:5-6). He finishes by emphasizing that the letter was written with his own hand – lending authority in case of any doubt.

NOTES & QUOTES:

In this letter, Paul again has to instruct the early Christians on the person of Christ, and his all-encompassing work of Grace amongst the believers.

The fact is that sometimes we need reminded that Jesus is ALL we need. Bells & smells, signs and wonders, dreams and visions, they all have their place. However they cannot replace a clear understanding of just exactly what salvation means, and the true benefits to us, of Jesus' sacrifice.

A clear understanding leads to a stronger faith, and better relationships that are not easily shaken when doubt or turmoil come visiting!

******

1 Thessalonians:

WHEN:
About A.D. 50-51

WHO:

The Apostle Paul (Possibly with additions from Silvanus & Timothy)

PEOPLE & PLACES:
Christ; Paul; Timothy; Silvanus
Thessalonica; Philippi

SOUND-BITES:
for our gospel did not come to you in word only, but also in power and in the Holy Spirit and with full conviction; just as you know what kind of men we proved to be among you for your sake. (Ch.1:5)

For the Lord Himself will descend from heaven with a shout, with the voice of the archangel and with the trumpet of God, and the dead in Christ will rise first. (Ch.4:16)

For God has not destined us for wrath, but for obtaining salvation through our Lord Jesus Christ. (Ch.5:9)

THE MESSIANIC LINK:
The Messiah rescues us from the wrath to come. (Ch.1:10)

THE BOOK:
Although Paul seems to spend the first 3 chapters recounting his previous dealings with the church, and his attempts to visit them earlier but for the work of Satan (Ch.2:18); the book in general is eschatologically based. All 5 chapters end with a reference to the second coming of Jesus.
From chapter 4 v 13 onwards, the subject of Christians dying before Jesus returns, leads to Paul explaining that

they will indeed play a part in the resurrection, and that we will all meet together in the clouds.

The final chapter encourages the believers to wait patiently, to be sober and alert (5;6), so that we are not surprised when the great day arrives 'like a thief in the night.' (Ch.5:2)

NOTES & QUOTES:

The early Church did have a bit of a problem with the 'second coming' of Jesus; they were getting older and some of them had passed away, but still Jesus had not appeared – what would happen to them?

Paul then gave them – and us – good advice... Be patient! The Lord has not forgotten those who have passed away, indeed they will be raised first (Ch.4:15). The only thing we have to concern ourselves with is to be alert and aware that we could be called into Glory at any moment – and never experience physical death (v17). Known as 'The Rapture of the Church;' this is a passage that should excite and enthuse any follower of Christ. Personally I can hardly wait!

******

2 Thessalonians:

WHEN:
About A.D. 50-51

WHO:

The Apostle Paul (Possibly with additions from Silvanus & Timothy)

PEOPLE & PLACES:
Christ; Paul; Timothy; Silvanus
Thessalonica

SOUND-BITES:
For the mystery of lawlessness is already at work; only he who now restrains will do so until he is taken out of the way. (Ch.2:7)

But the Lord is faithful, and He will strengthen and protect you from the evil one. (Ch.3:3)

But as for you, brethren, do not grow weary of doing good. (Ch.3:13)

THE MESSIANIC LINK:
The Messiah is the Lord of Peace. (Ch.3:16)

THE BOOK:
The Thessalonian church was still plagued by persecution and misunderstanding at this time, hence this second letter is written just shortly after the first.
Again it Paul concentrates on clearing up the events leading up to the 'Second Coming,' and instructs the believers on what must happen before such events can come to pass.
The second chapter concentrates on the 'man of lawlessness' (Ch.2:3-9) and the apostasy that will mark his time here on Earth.

He exhorts them in chapter 3 to live an upright life and not to weary in doing good deeds and working for a living; using himself as an example in this matter.
He concludes by pointing out that the letter has been written by his own hand, so that they may recognize it and grant it due authority.

Notes & Quotes:

The writings to the Thessalonian church are a timely reminder that although it is right to expect The Lord to come back soon; it is not right just to give up everything and sit down to wait for him!
Many things must first come to pass, such as the appearance of the character Paul calls the 'man of lawlessness' also known as the antichrist (2 John 1:7).
Meanwhile, life goes on and we must focus on worshiping The Lord, and going about our everyday business, while at the same time keeping alert for signs of the 'end days;' if we are to keep things in a proper balance.

******

1 Timothy:

When:
Around A.D.64

Who:
The Apostle Paul

People & Places:

Christ; Paul; Timothy
Ephesus; Macedonia

SOUND-BITES:

It is a trustworthy statement, deserving full acceptance, that Christ Jesus came into the world to save sinners, among whom I am foremost of all. (Ch.1:15)

For there is one God, and one mediator also between God and men, the man Christ Jesus. (Ch.2:5)

For the love of money is a root of all sorts of evil, and some by longing for it have wandered away from the faith and pierced themselves with many griefs. (Ch.6:10)

Fight the good fight of faith; take hold of the eternal life to which you were called, and you made the good confession in the presence of many witnesses. (Ch.6:12)

THE MESSIANIC LINK:

Messiah is the Mediator between God and men. (1 Timothy 2:5)

THE BOOK:

In this letter Paul begins by warning Timothy regarding false teachers; instructs the young pastor on the running of a church, and how to deal with issues such as appointing Deacons or Elders from within the congregation.
In Chapter 4 he warns Timothy to watch out for Apostasy in the later times; and also instructs him on discipline, and how he should treat the widows within the church in chapter 5.

He concludes the letter with more instruction on leadership, and warning him that the love of money is the root of all sorts of evil, so to be rich in good works thereby building up a 'treasure of good foundation.'

NOTES & QUOTES:

This letter to Timothy forms an excellent instruction manual on setting up a new church, as it covers church leadership, discipline and administration; and all in only 6 chapters! Even for those not involved in leadership issues though, there is excellent instruction here on avoiding false teachers and how to contend for the faith in everyday life.

******

2 Timothy:

WHEN:
Around A.D. 66

WHO:
The Apostle Paul

PEOPLE & PLACES:
Christ: Paul; Timothy; Onesiphorus
Ephesus

SOUND-BITES:
All Scripture is inspired by God and profitable for teaching, for reproof, for correction, for training in righteousness. (Ch.3:16)

Preach the word; be ready in season and out of season; reprove, rebuke, exhort, with great patience and instruction. (Ch.4:2)

I have fought the good fight, I have finished the course, I have kept the faith. (Ch.4:7)

THE MESSIANIC LINK:
He is the descendant of David and the Saviour. (Ch.2:8,10)

THE BOOK:
2 Timothy was written near the end of Paul's life, as he lay imprisoned for a second time in Rome. He begins this letter by encouraging his 'beloved son' Timothy, to keep strong in the Faith, and not to succumb to a 'spirit of timidity.' Chapter 2 relates the sufferings that Paul himself has endured for the Gospel's sake, as he encourages Timothy not to be ashamed (v15), but to accurately preach the word, avoiding needless quarrel and false teachers.
The last two chapters cover instruction on the difficult times ahead, as people become 'lovers of self;' persecution comes, and people will not accept 'sound doctrine' (Ch.4:3).
Paul finishes by warning Timothy against Alexander the coppersmith, who opposed him severely; and asks Timothy to try to visit him before winter sets in.

NOTES & QUOTES:
Paul wrote this letter during the time of the Megalomaniac Emperor Nero, and while he was languishing in jail. By all accounts he knew that he did not have long for this world; he had 'fought the good fight' and it was almost time for

him to be called home and receive his 'crown of righteousness.'

How many of us I wonder, would be able to maintain this positive mental attitude, while imprisoned and awaiting death? And yet Paul still expresses a real concern for others – especially Timothy and the young church - during this time.

I'd like to say I would be exactly the same; but the truth is I would probably be too busy making my own plans to escape!

******

Titus:

WHEN:
Around A.D.66

WHO:
The Apostle Paul (1:1)

PEOPLE & PLACES:
Christ; Paul; Titus
Crete; Nicopolis

SOUND-BITES:
They profess to know God, but by their deeds they deny Him, being detestable and disobedient and worthless for any good deed. (Ch.1:16)

Who gave Himself for us to redeem us from every lawless deed, and to purify for Himself a people for His own possession, zealous for good deeds. (Ch.2:14)

But when the kindness of God our Savior and His love for mankind appeared, **5.** He saved us, not on the basis of deeds which we have done in righteousness, but according to His mercy, by the washing of regeneration and renewing by the Holy Spirit. (Ch.3:4-5)

THE MESSIANIC LINK:
He is the Blessed Hope, and our Great God and Saviour. (Titus 2:13)

THE BOOK:
This letter to Titus is similar to Pauls writing to Timothy, in that he is instructing a young Pastor in the fine details of dealing with church life and ministry. He lays down the qualifications for elders and warns against the false teachers and rebellious men in the first chapter.

In the second chapter Paul covers acceptable Christian behaviour and family life, urging Titus himself to lead by good example; and not to shy from using his authority to 'exhort and reprove.' (Ch.2:15)

Paul finishes his letter by expressing some personal concerns regarding the needs of individuals within the church, and asks Titus to visit him at Nicopolis as soon as he is able.

NOTES & QUOTES:
As in the letters to Timothy, Paul really shows his 'Pastors heart' in this letter to Titus. This is a church that Paul

himself had recently set up, and had now left in the care of his 'child in the faith' Titus. However, although he had left Titus in charge, he had not abandoned him to his own devices, and was still helping him out with the many issues involved with running a new church.

This is indeed true discipleship, and a lesson in how to treat not just a new church, but a new Christian. The Great Commission of Mathew 28:19 after all does not call us to make 'converts' but rather to make 'disciples.'

******

Philemon:

WHEN:
Written in A.D. 60

WHO:
The Apostle Paul

PEOPLE & PLACES:
Christ; Paul; Timothy; Philemon; Apphia; Archippus; Onesimus; Colosse

SOUND-BITES:
I thank my God always, making mention of you in my prayers. (Ch.1:4)

no longer as a slave, but more than a slave, a beloved brother, especially to me, but how much more to you, both in the flesh and in the Lord. (Ch.1:16)

The Messianic Link:
The Lord Jesus Christ (V. 3)

The Book:
This is the shortest of Paul's letters, and covers one subject in the main; that of the runaway slave Onesimus.

He writes directly to Philemon who was a Christian, but also a slave-owner; as were other Christians at this early time.

The crux of Pauls appeal is that Onesimus is not only a personal friend of the Apostle, but that he is also now a brother in Christ (v16); and should perhaps be considered in a different light.

Notes & Quotes:
Paul in this short letter confronts what was a difficult issue for the early Church. Slavery was a fact of life throughout the World at this time, and Christians did indeed possess slaves. In other letter Paul instructs slaves to obey their masters, and masters to be fair to their slaves (Eph.6, Colossians 3), because God was watching and would take all things into account.

Onesimus was a different case only inasmuch as he had become a Christian, and at the same time befriended Paul, who was then able to appeal on his behalf. The penalty for a runaway slave was death.

This is an excellent example of what Jesus does for Christians, he appeals to God the Father on our behalf because the penalty for our sins was death; but now we have eternal life in Him. (Rom.6:23)

******

Hebrews:

WHEN:
Around A.D. 65-70

WHO:
Unknown, but Apollos or Barnabas most likely

PEOPLE & PLACES:
Christ; Melchizedek; Moses

SOUND-BITES:
How will we escape if we neglect so great a salvation? After it was at the first spoken through the Lord, it was confirmed to us by those who heard. (Ch.2:3)

Therefore, since we have a great high priest who has passed through the heavens, Jesus the Son of God, let us hold fast our confession. (Ch.4:14)

So much the more also Jesus has become the guarantee of a better covenant. (Ch.7:22)

Now faith is the [a]assurance of things hoped for, the conviction of things not seen. (Ch.11:1)

Jesus Christ is the same yesterday and today and forever. (Ch.13:8)

THE MESSIANIC LINK:
He is the Heir of All Things (Hebrews 1:2)

The Merciful & Faithful High Priest (Hebrews 2:17)
The Author and Finisher of our Faith (Hebrews 12:2)

THE BOOK:

The book of Hebrews was written primarily to Jews who had converted to Christianity, but were now perhaps a little unsure as to the person of Christ.

Jesus is portrayed throughout as the perfect revelation of God and superior to Angels, Moses, Melchizedek or the Priesthood; and indeed was the Perfect Sacrifice that instituted the New Covenant. (Chaps 5-10)

The author frequently appeals to the Torah to re-enforce their claims, as in the case of Melchizedek (Ch.7), as the Jews would be familiar with these scriptures.

From chapter 10 onward the writer warns of the perils of falling away, and reverting to the old, broken system of sacrifice that was only ever a temporary measure until the perfect sacrifice had come. (Ch.10:14)

The last chapters continue to emphasize the efficacy of Jesus, and to encourage the believers to meditate on and believe what he has told them.

NOTES & QUOTES:

There is no doubt that the book of Hebrews is one of the 'big hitters' in the New Testament; for in it there is a great wealth of information regarding the person of Christ, and just how exactly he was indeed the perfect sacrifice able to cover our sins.

There is also a lot to be said about the pearl of unbelief, or falling away from the faith. These passages must be approached with great consideration as to just who they are aimed at; believers, intellectual believers, or wannabees who had made a confession of sorts, but when persecution came, had rejected Christ.

******

James:

WHEN:
Around A.D. 45-48

WHO:
James (brother of Jesus)

PEOPLE & PLACES:
Christ; James; Elijah

SOUND-BITES:
Consider it all joy, my brethren, when you encounter various trials, **3.** knowing that the testing of your faith produces endurance. (Ch.1:2-3)

But prove yourselves doers of the word, and not merely hearers who delude themselves. (Ch.1:22)

Even so faith, if it has no works, is dead, being by itself. (Ch.2:17)

So also the tongue is a small part of the body, and yet it boasts of great things. See how great a forest is set aflame by such a small fire! (Ch.3:5)

The Messianic Link:
The Judge standing at the door (James 5:9)

The Book:
This book is written not to an individual church, but to Christians in general.

It begins by emphasizing the trials and temptations that will come, and the importance of 'putting aside' the old self, and adopting the new.

Chapter 2 gives teaching on the importance of not showing favouritism amongst certain members of the church; as well as emphasizing that faith without works is a dead faith.

Chapter 3 onwards instructs on Christian behaviour in regard to speech, avoiding jealousy, immorality and the misuse of wealth; especially the crime of withholding wages from the workers.

The book finishes with an exhortation to pray for the sick, and to confess their sins to one another.

Notes & Quotes:
The great reformer Martin Luther referred to this letter as 'The epistle of straw,' because he could not reconcile it with the Apostle Pauls teachings on salvation by faith alone.

The book of James seems to fly in the face of this doctrine, when he says that 'faith without works is dead' (Ch.2:26); the whole letter seems to emphasise this point, much to the detriment of 'Pauls gospel.'

However, this is not the case, and is easily reconciled by considering that although Salvation is indeed by Grace and faith alone - according to a reading of the full Gospel in proper context - good works can be regarded as the outward sign of a living faith – though not necessarily evidence of it.

******

1 Peter:

WHEN:
Around A.D. 64

WHO:
The Apostle Peter (Ch.1:1)

PEOPLE & PLACES:
Christ; Peter; Silvanus; Mark
Galatia; Cappadocia; Asia

SOUND-BITES:
But you are a chosen race, a royal priesthood, a holy nation, a people for God's own possession, so that you may proclaim the excellencies of Him who has called you out of darkness into His marvelous light. (Ch.2:9)

And He Himself bore our sins in His body on the cross, so that we might die to sin and live to righteousness; for by His wounds you were healed. (Ch.2:24)

Be of sober spirit, be on the alert. Your adversary, the devil, prowls around like a roaring lion, seeking someone to devour. (Ch.5:8)

The Messianic Link:
He is the Living Stone (1 Peter 2:4)
The Chief Shepherd (1 Peter 5:4)

The Book:
In this letter Peter addresses the persecutions and the sufferings that the believers have been enduring for the gospels sake, as well as encouraging them to stay strong in the faith and to 'be holy' (Ch.1:15-16).

He emphasizes the fact that they are a 'chosen race' and a 'royal priesthood,' and that their behaviour must be exemplary amongst the unbelievers in order to give a good witness for the Faith (Ch2:12), that people may see this and glorify God.

Chapter 4 exhorts them to discard their previous 'lusts of men' and instead to live instead for the will of God, for the end of this age is near. The trials that they are undergoing should be no surprise to them, because they are indeed sharing in the sufferings of Christ in this matter.

He finishes this book with the warning that they must beware of their adversary the devil, and to resist him by being strong in the faith.

Notes & Quotes:
Peter has much to say in this letter regarding various doctrines and Christian behaviour, especially with regard to being a credible witness for the gospel.

He was however mainly writing in order to encourage the early church during a period of intense persecution, and at a time when it was much easier to drift away and live a carnal, ungodly life.

Peter warns us to be on guard against the devil, who is the real adversary behind the scenes; whose tactics are pretty much the same as they always were. If he cannot discourage us with persecutions, then he can offer many other inducements in order to distract us from our ultimate goal of simply worshiping the Lord Jesus, and expectantly awaiting his return.

******

2 Peter:

WHEN:
Written about A.D.66

WHO:
The Apostle Peter

PEOPLE & PLACES:
Christ; Peter; Paul

SOUND-BITES:
For we did not follow cleverly devised tales when we made known to you the power and coming of our Lord Jesus Christ, but we were eyewitnesses of His majesty. (Ch.1:16)

Promising them freedom while they themselves are slaves of corruption; for by what a man is overcome, by this he is enslaved. (Ch.2:19)

The Lord is not slow about His promise, as some count slowness, but is patient toward you, not wishing for any to perish but for all to come to repentance. (Ch.3:9)

The Messianic Link:
He is the Beloved Son (Ch.1:17)

The Book:
Peter begins his letter by reminding the believers of his earlier ministrations concerning Christian behaviour, and the person of Christ. False prophets and teachers were posing a problem at this time, so Peter warns them throughout the second chapter to be aware of such people; advising amongst other things that these people are 'slaves of corruption' (2:19), and to be avoided at all costs.

In the last chapter he counters the false teachers who say that the Lord is not coming back at all, and reminds them that God's timing is not the same as ours, and indeed 1000 of our years is only a day to Him.

He ends the book by again exhorting them to be alert to false teachings, especially those who would attempt to distort the teachings of the Apostle Paul, whose writings are sometimes difficult to grasp (Ch.3:15-16).

Notes & Quotes:
False teachers and disinformation campaigns have always been one of the enemy's biggest ploys, in his battle to undermine the work of Christ and discredit His people. Interestingly it is a ploy that has been used by various governments and peoples since time began, to confuse and defeat their enemies. Disinformation is a very powerful

weapon in times of war, and helps keep the opposition 'on the back foot' so to speak.

As Paul tells us in the book of Ephesians (6:12), we are in a time of spiritual warfare so we should not be surprised that the devil uses disinformation and false teaching to try and undermine the true Faith, thereby weakening our resolve to be effective witness for The Lord.

******

1 John:

WHEN:
Most likely between A.D.85 – 95

WHO:
The Apostle John

PEOPLE & PLACES:
Jesus Christ

SOUND-BITES:
If we confess our sins, He is faithful and righteous to forgive us our sins and to cleanse us from all unrighteousness. (Ch.1:9)

Beloved, do not believe every spirit, but test the spirits to see whether they are from God, because many false prophets have gone out into the world. (Ch.4:1)

He who has the Son has the life; he who does not have the Son of God does not have the life. (Ch.5:12)

THE MESSIANIC LINK:
The 'Eternal Life' of Ch.1:2
The Advocate with the Father (Ch. 2:1)

THE BOOK:
John wrote this book with the intention of stopping the influence of false teachers, and in particular the teachers of Gnosticism that were hounding the new believers. John proclaims from the beginning that 'God is light,' as a way of highlighting the dark immoral teachings of the Gnostics and encouraging the believers to walk in the light of The Lord.

He continues this letter by re-iterating the basic tenants of the faith, emphasizing that he did not expect them to be perfect (1:9), but that they should overcome the world by showing their love for one another as God loves us; by loving God and keeping his commandments (5:3).
He finishes the letter by encouraging the believers that they have eternal life already through Christ, who has given them understanding so that they may know the truth.

NOTES & QUOTES:
The Apostle John was particularly concerned with the influence of the Gnostic's within the church, who basically advocated that all spirit was good and all flesh was bad, there-fore Jesus was not a real physical being but a spirit-being. Not only did John deal with this very effectively, but he also gave us this terrific epistle on love; and just what it really should be like between ourselves and between us and God the Father.

John teaches us here that by keeping our eyes on Jesus and by following his commandments to love one another, then we can indeed 'overcome the world' and walk in the light of the true Gospel of Christ.

******

2 John:

WHEN:
Around A.D. 85-95

WHO:
The Apostle John

PEOPLE & PLACES:
Jesus Christ

SOUND-BITES:
For many deceivers have gone out into the world, those who do not acknowledge Jesus Christ as coming in the flesh. This is the deceiver and the antichrist. (Ch.1:7)

THE MESSIANIC LINK:
He is the Truth which abides in us. (Ch1:2)

THE BOOK:
In this short letter of only one chapter, John is again most concerned about the false Gnostic teachers who are pestering the church. He advises that the easiest way to catch them out is to ask them if Christ came in the flesh; if

they deny that this was so, then they are deceivers and the antichrist. (v7)

Such people should not be accepted or allowed into their house, as to do so would be to participate in their sin.

NOTES & QUOTES:

There was a campaign 'doing the rounds' at this time, seeking to undermine the eye witness accounts of Jesus physical resurrection. These accounts basically claimed that it was not Jesus at all, But his ghost or spirit. John and the other Apostles – who were there at the time - refute this vehemently

Even today I have heard Jesus described as all sorts of things, from a spirit-man to a nice man to space-man! However only acknowledgement that Jesus was indeed the Son of God, crucified and risen in the flesh; will be enough to satisfy The Father that we are worthy to enter the kingdom of Heaven, and participate in the marriage supper of The Lamb (Rev.19:7-9).

******

3 John:

WHEN:
Around A.D. 90-95

WHO:
The Apostle John

PEOPLE & PLACES:

Gaius; Demetrius; Diotrephes;

SOUND-BITES:

Beloved, do not imitate what is evil, but what is good. The one who does good is of God; the one who does evil has not seen God. (v.11)

THE MESSIANIC LINK:

He is *The Name* in verse 7

THE BOOK:

John is writing to his friend Gaius, to wish him and the fellow believers well. However he is concerned about the leader Diotrephes, who will not allow John's messengers access to the church.

He finishes this short epistle by commending Demetrius to them, and advises them that he will soon come and deal with the matter 'face to face.'

NOTES & QUOTES:

Even people in leadership must subject themselves to leadership or oversight, for "power corrupts, and absolute power corrupts absolutely." Any church or individual who will not accept the advice of their appointed leaders within the movement; risks falling into the error and snare of 'the power trap.' For that reason alone it is not advisable for a church to be run by one man or woman – answerable to no-one but themselves - lest they should fall into this trap, and be led into error.

******

Jude:

WHEN:
Around A.D.65

WHO:
Jude, brother of James (Ch.1:1)

PEOPLE & PLACES:
Christ; Jude; James

Egypt; Sodom & Gomorrah;

SOUND-BITES:
Beloved, while I was making every effort to write you about our common salvation, I felt the necessity to write to you appealing that you contend earnestly for the faith which was once for all handed down to the saints. (v.3)

That they were saying to you, "In the last time there will be mockers, following after their own ungodly lusts." (v.18)

THE MESSIANIC LINK:
Messiah is Him who is able (v.24)

THE BOOK:
Jude begins his letter by saying he wanted to talk to them about their common salvation, but instead found it necessary to warn them about the false teachings and immoral behaviour that had infiltrated the church.
He continues by expressing his strong condemnation regarding these 'mockers' and 'worldly minded' people,

and advises the believers to build themselves up in the 'most holy faith,' by praying in the Holy Spirit (v.20).

NOTES & QUOTES:

This letter was written by 'Jude the brother of James,' who is also believed to be Judas, the brother of our Lord Jesus. Immorality amongst believers is something that must be guarded against at all costs, and the lust of this world replaced with the true love of God; if a church or individual Christian is to see victory over temptation of all kinds. We live in an age where sex is used to sell just about everything you can imagine, from shampoo to chocolate. This is an age that promotes promiscuity at a whole different level; I'm fairly convinced that Jude's letter would have been a lot longer if he were writing it today. (Said tongue-in-cheek!)

******

Revelation:

WHEN:
Written around A.D. 95

WHO:
The Apostle John

PEOPLE & PLACES:
Christ; John; Michael; Satan; The Beast; Angels
Babylon; Ephesus; Smyrna; Pergamum; Thyatira; Sardis;
Philadelphia; Laodicea; Heaven

SOUND-BITES:

"I am the Alpha and the Omega," says the Lord God, "who is and who was and who is to come, the Almighty." (Ch.1:8)

Behold, I stand at the door and knock; if anyone hears My voice and opens the door, I will come in to him and will dine with him, and he with Me. (Ch.3:20)

Here is wisdom. Let him who has understanding calculate the number of the beast, for the number is that of a man; and his number is six hundred and sixty-six. (Ch.13:18)

Then I saw a great white throne and Him who sat upon it, from whose presence earth and heaven fled away, and no place was found for them. (Ch.20:11)

THE MESSIANIC LINK:

The First and the Last (Ch.1:17)
The Lion from the Tribe of Judah (Ch.5:5)
The Lamb that was slain (Ch.5:12)
The Word of God (Ch.19:13) and the King of kings and Lord of lords (Ch.19:16)
The Bright Morning Star (Ch.22:16)

THE BOOK:

The book of revelation starts with a warning to the seven churches scattered throughout the known world at that time; and follows a general theme, emphasizing that the 'end of days' is near and that the church must be prepared for the events that are to come.

In graphic and figurative form, John describes the breaking of the seven seals (Chaps. 6-8); and the devastation that follows. The seven headed dragon and the beast from the sea and from the earth (Ch.13); and the doom waiting for the bearers of his mark or number (666).

The seven 'bowls of wrath' and the fall of Babylon are described in graphic detail in Chaps 17,18.

Chapter 19 relates the 'marriage supper of The Lamb' and the coming of Christ to wage war on the beast and his followers. Satan is bound then freed again in chapter 20, in order to face his final judgement; along with the unbelievers in the great white throne Judgement of God.

Chapters 21-22 finish with a vision of the new Heaven and Earth, where there is no longer any curse of death or pain or suffering; and God himself rules the Kingdom in perfect harmony and peace.

Notes & Quotes:

The book of Revelations it must be admitted, is perhaps not the lightest read in the Bible! In fact a lot of people find it both confusing and frightening, heavily accentuated as it is with allegory and terrifying visions of locusts with a sting like scorpion's and teeth like the teeth of lions; and other no-less terrifying accounts of dragons & plagues; disease and pestilence.

Are all these things for real? Well the Apostle John certainly seemed to think so, and indeed he was instructed to record these visions in the first verse and in the last chapter of the book, by the Angel of The Lord.

In my own opinion, these visions are meant to frighten and scare people – because the Judgement at the 'end of days' is a frightening prospect for those who do not know Christ, or have not repented and accepted him as their saviour.

Am I saying then that we should be scaring people into the kingdom of Heaven? Hmmm, perhaps scaring them out of Hell would be a better way of putting it. The fact remains though, that there is a Judgement day coming; and by all accounts it is not that far away!

******

A Personal Conclusion

Firstly let me just thank you for purchasing my book – it is very much appreciated.

When it came to writing this work, the hardest part was trying to summarise in a few words, the main lessons or highlights of the particular books involved; and if this happens to be a book the size of Leviticus or perhaps any of the major prophets – then I have no doubt that I have failed miserably!

Everyone will have a different opinion as to what the main part or lesson of any of these wonderful books is exactly, but hopefully this limited work will encourage you to find out your own favourite passage, phrase, story or character – if you have not already done so.

When it comes to accurately dating the individual books, then this also is open to debate in most instances, and so I have included the dates that in my mind are most supported by the Bible itself.

Finally, if you think that this work is biased towards a literal interpretation of the events within the Bible – I can confirm that this is indeed the case – interpretation is not required when the facts are plainly written, and allegory is not intended.

As for the sections on 'The Book,' and the 'Notes & Quotes.' These are my own perhaps not-so-humble opinions! I offer them to you as suggestions and opinions entirely my own, and not in any way to be taken as 'divine authority' so to speak.

******

Other Books In This Series: 'Spotlight On'

Book 1: Spotlight On The Minor Prophets: Bible Study Guide (Old Testament Prophets) - 6 Book Bundle (1): Jonah, Obadiah, Joel, Hosea, Amos, Micah [Kindle Edition]

Book 2: Spotlight On The Minor Prophets: Bible Study Guide (Old Testament Prophets) - 6 Book Bundle (2): Nahum, Zephaniah, Habakkuk, Haggai, Zechariah, Malachi [Kindle Edition]

Book 3: Spotlight On The Minor Prophets: Bible Study Guide - 12 Book Bundle (Old Testament Prophets Study Guide) [Kindle Edition]

******

Made in the USA
Lexington, KY
29 December 2012